A PRACTICAL GUIDE
for the
GENEALOGIST IN ENGLAND

By RACHAEL MELLEN

HERITAGE BOOKS
1986

Published By

HERITAGE BOOKS, INC.
3602 Maureen Lane, Bowie, MD 20715
phone (301)-464-1159

ISBN 0-917890-85-X

This book is dedicated to the memory of my mother
Betty Butler 1916-1984

ACKNOWLEDGEMENTS

There are so many people without whose generous assistance and encouragement this book would not have been written: primarily my husband, Robert, and children, Elizabeth and Robin. Barb Harl patiently typed the manuscript, several times, and my sister Ruth Dipple helped with snippets of research.

Many thanks go to Alan Crosby for the beautiful maps in Chapters 4 and 5, and to Mr. A. M. Wherry and Miss Jean Kennedy of the Hereford and Worcester and Norfolk Record Offices for granting permission to reproduce records in their jurisdiction. Finally, thanks go to Karen Ackermann for her thoughtful and perceptive suggestions which allowed the book to take a readable shape.

TABLE OF CONTENTS

TABLE OF CONTENTS

INTRODUCTION

1980. A cool July day in a remote village in County Durham. My nephew and I spent the morning combing the parish cemetery for Bonds and Turners, ancestors of my husband, with some success on the Bond side. An inquiry in the local grocery shop sent us on a visit to the retired school-teacher, the authority on local history. She happened to be living on property once owned by my husband's ancestors and she took us to the gentleman who now owned the Bond Foundry. Interesting, to be sure, but not sensational!

I decided to head for the parish church to ask about examing the burial records. It was a Saturday and a little old lady, Miss Gill, was arranging flowers for a wedding. I asked her about reading the registers and discovered that the priest was in Burham all morning, much to my disappointment. (Moral: Never ask to search registers on a Saturday.)

The lady asked me why I was interested in the parish registers; I told her I was searching for the burial of Abraham Turner. Her face lit up: "Old Abraham Turner! Why yes, when I was a little girl I saw a painting of him in his guards' uniform."

Eureka!

Miss Gill was only too eager to explain that she had regularly, as a young girl, visited Abraham Turner's widow, who was born a Bond. She remembered Mrs. Turner as a china doll lady dressed in black, with white hair and a lace cap. As we came out of the church, Miss Gill showed my nephew and me the house where Mrs. Turner had died. Miss Gill, the daughter of a foreman in the Bond foundry, filled me in on many little details of the family and local history. Even though this was only 'hearsay' evidence, it confirmed other evidence and stimulated my desire to find out more. To see and be there - that is the stuff of living family history.

Two years later, I re-visited Miss Gill with my American husband, great-great-great grandson of Mrs. Turner, so that he could hear Miss Gill's stories himself. We had tea in her drawing room overlooking the Pennines and the family returned to its origins.

Not everyone who visits England in search of their ancestry will be thus rewarded but the prospects of a rich harvest are great. With proper preparation and realistic objectives, you can locate valuable docmentary evidence, acquire a true appreciation of your ancestors' homeland, perhaps contact distant relatives, and certainly make new friends. This manual will attempt to aid you in your preparations and guide you in your searches.

1

CHAPTER 1

THE BASICS OF ENGLISH GENEALOGY

Genealogy is an increasingly popular hobby, particularly since the Bicentennial celebrations and the publication of Roots by Alex Haley. Haley's book has given encouragement to many to trace their family's history even though they may have come from a very humble background. Genealogy now has a mass appeal.

So where do you begin? How will you organize your findings? What do you need to know about English history and geography? In this chapter, I will answer these questions sequentially.

Where To Begin

Genealogical research always goes from the known to the unknown. Your first task is to collect data on yourself: weed out your birth and marriage certificates, and any diaries, letters, or journals you may have kept. Get your children's certificates, too. You are now ready to fill in a Family Group Sheet. See Fig. 1A.

The Family Group Sheet outlines three generations. It is a very important tool as it summarizes at a glance the status of your research. There are spaces for all the basic facts about one couple, including vital statistics on their parents and their children. Note the space for sources at the bottom; this will remind you where your information came from and allows you to double-check at a later time and avoid repetitious research. When you are certain your facts are correct, use ink; if in doubt, use pencil.

Branching Out

Having collected as much about yourself as possible, the next step is to interview (in person or by letter), all your older relatives. This can be difficult if the relative is in ill-health or if some family feud is still smouldering, but you will probably be surprised at how pleased many old folks are in the interest you express in their parents and grandparents.

Take along a tape-recorder if possible; you can then have a fairly natural conversation without seeming like a news-reporter. Jot down a list of questions about the subject's family beforehand, but don't feel compelled to stick religiously to the list. Rambling diversions can sometimes lead to important clues. Be aware that there may be a 'skeleton in the closet', which, even after many years, a person is still anxious to hide. Respect their right to privacy. It will make your research more challenging, but it pays to be tactful.

Sometimes the subject may not be aware of the 'skeleton': I could never garner any information from my grandmother about her father-in-law except that he died accidently in 1911. Later research revealed he was illegitimate - a fact he probably tried to 'forget'.

Fig. 1A   FAMILY GROUP SHEET

Name and address of researcher:

Husband's name:	Wife's name:
Born - place & date:	Born - place & date:
Married - place & date:	Died - place & date:
Died - place & date:	
Husband's father:	Wife's father:
Born - place & date:	Born - place & date:
Married - place & date:	Married - place & date:
Died - place & date:	Died - place & date:
Husband's mother:	Wife's mother:
Born - place & date:	Born - place & date:
Died - place & date:	Died - place & date:

Other date about husband: religion _____ occupation _____ names of other wives _____

Children

Name	Sex	Date of birth of baptism	Place	Spouse's name & date of marriage	Date of death or burial	Place
1.						
2.						
3.						
4.						
5.						
6.						
7.						
8.						
9.						
10.						
11.						
12.						
13.						

Sources:

Family Documents

By the time you have interviewed all possible relatives, you may have also acquired photographs, letters, diaries, certificates of birth, baptism, marriage and death, plus family bibles, passports, and other family documents. These are important in confirming the oral facts you have heard and can be divided into two catagories:

a) Primary sources: written by the people involved or someone who was there. In this category come wills, letters, diaries, birth/marriage certificates, school reports, etc. These documents have greater reliability and credibility than secondary sources because they are first-hand evidence.

b) Secondary sources: written by people who were not eyewitnesses to events referred to in the documents. In this category come obituaries (which often describe events that took place before the informant's own birth), death certificates, family bible records (to some extent), oral history, and newspaper reports. These sources may not be totally reliable and must, if possible, be backed up by a primary source. It is for this reason that genealogists become so involved in searching for birth and marriage certificates and, in an earlier period, church records of baptisms, weddings, and burials.

Documenting Your Findings

Now begin to build a framework of the solid evidence which you have unearthed about your family members. The Pedigree Chart is a map of the family, the sign posts being your direct ancestors. (See Figure 1B.) Begin on the left with #1 (yourself) and work across to the right, filling in as much data as you can. Use pencil if you are not sure of your facts.

Names should always be written thus: John SMITH. If the person was better known by a nickname, write this in parentheses: John (Kipper) SMITH. Dates are always written with the number first, then month abbreviated in capitals, and the year in full. For example, 10 APR 1852.

Pedigree charts are standard amongst genealogists. Later you may find yourself exchanging charts with hitherto unkown relatives, so make sure you follow the standard formula.

After the chart is filled in, your next step is to recheck the information on each generation by gathering the necessary birth, marriage, and death certificates. In the USA, vital statistic registration is a comparatively new innovation; in Illinois, for example, it was not compulsory until 1916. To find out when your state began registration, call the county clerk's office or write to the U.S. Government Printing Office, Superintendent of Documents, Washington DC 20402 and ask for the pamphlet, Where to Write for Birth, Marriage and Death Certificates; this lists addresses for each state, record dates, and certificate costs.

Due to the relatively late arrival of vital statistic registration in the United States, you may find it necessary to visit and/or write to churches in the towns in which your ancestors lived. Many churches have records dating from the early nineteenth century, some go back to the eighteenth century. But beware! The records may be written in Latin, German, Polish, Italian, or French, depending on the nationality of the immigrant group which they served. NOTE: Some churches do not allow record searching. In such a case, tact and patience are the researcher's main assests, but it may be necessary to rely on diaries, probate, or guardianship records. You cannot force an institution to show its records.

Wills are an important primary source. Leaving a will has been a much more common practice in the United States than in Britain, due to the fact that more people were property-holders in the U.S. Wills and other probate documents can name a large proportion of the deceased's family and include such facts

4

Fig. 1B PEDIGREE CHART

Name and address of compiler:

Chart #___

Name:
B or X:
Where:
Married:
Where:
Died/buried:
Where:

Spouse:
B or X:
Where:
Died/buried:
Where:

2. Name:
B or X:
Where:
Married:
Where:
Died/buried:
Where:

3. Name:
B or X:
Where:
Died/buried:
Where:

4. Name:
B or X:
Where:
Married:
Where:
Died/buried:
Where:

5. Name:
B or X:
Where:
Died/buried:
Where:

6. Name:
B or X:
Where:
Married:
Where:
Died/buried:
Where:

7. Name:
B or X:
Where:
Died/buried:
Where:

8. Name:
B or X:
Married:
Died/buried:

9. Name:
B or X:
Died/buried:

10. Name:
B or X:
Married:
Died/buried:

11. Name:
B or X:
Died/buried:

12. Name:
B or X:
Married:
Died/buried:

13. Name:
B or X:
Died/buried

14. Name:
B or X:
Married:
Died/buried:

15. Name:
B or X:
Died/buried:

16.
17.
18.
19.
20.
21.
22.
23.
24.
25.
26.
27.
28.
29.
30.
31.

B = Born   X = Christened

as the deceased's name, residence and date of death, list of property and heirs, testators and executors. Since photostat copies are relatively inexpensive, a copy of a probate record would be a better 'buy' than a death certificate. (Death certificates usually contain the following facts: deceased's name, date and place of birth, cause and date of death, deceased's parents' names. However, these details vary between states and are likely to be less complete before the 20th century.)

One major source of secondary information is the cemetery inscription. Although the amount of information varies enormously from stone to stone, the inscription can give you some unexpected leads and it is important to find out if a tombstone exists. Copy the inscription verbatim, even apparent misspelling and, if possible, take a photograph. (See Chapter 6). Vandalism and erosion may eliminate this source if you wait too long!

Finding Out Where Your Ancestors Came From

By now you have probably reached back to the nineteenth century or even earlier. From tombstones, letters, or oral tradition you may have a good idea whence your ancestors emigrated and when. How can you confirm this? There are three main sources:

a) Censuses, taken every ten years since 1790 (except 1940), have become more and more detailed. Before 1850, censuses listed only the head of household by name; the rest of the family and servants or slaves were categorized by sex and age, and were not named. The early censuses therefore have a more limited use, especially as country of origin was not noted. Since 1850, the censuses have shown the place of birth (usually given as a state or county); since 1880, the birthplace of parents has been given; on the 1900 and 1910 censuses immigrants had to state their year of arrival. (Unfortunately, the 1890 census was almost completely destroyed by fire.) If you do not know where your ancestors were residing in 1900 or 1910 there is a Soundex (index) on microfilm which can be consulted through interlibrary loan. Libraries can also obtain microfilm of the census this way.

b) Naturalization records were held at county courthouses until the formation of the Immigration and Naturalization Service in 1906. Prior to 1906 information obtained in records was so sketchy as to be worthless genealogically; after that date, however, much fuller statements were required. Thus, after 1906, naturalization papers gave the petitioner's name, address, last address in the country of origin, birthplace, parents' names (including mother's maiden name), port of entry into the U.S., and date of entry. Copies of declarations of intention and petitions for naturalization may be obtained by sending for form N-585 from the Immigration and Naturalization Service, 119 D Street NW, Washington DC 20536, and returning it with the appropriate fee.

c) Ships' passenger lists and customs records: provide the most complete information on the immigrant. After 1820, this included name, last residence, age, occupation, port of embarkation, and destination in the United States. Some ports have been fully indexed, 1820-1874 New York (the busiest!) is indexed only for 1820-1846 and 1883-1906. If your ancestor came between 1846 and 1883, you need to know the exact date and name of the vessel - or be prepared to search miles of microfilm! The passenger index microfilms can be consulted at branches of the National Archives, established regionally.

I was fortunate enough to find an ancestor on the New York index, so I filled out Form 81 (11-84) for a copy of the complete record from the National Archives, only to be told that the original list had been lost. A great disappointment.

Help! Where In England Did My Ancestors Come From?

Perhaps you can only establish that your family is from England, or perhaps you are more fortunate and have a particular county of origin. How can you establish which town or parish was your ancestor's birthplace? This is another situation akin to searching for a needle in a haystack, but help is at hand, thanks in most part to the Church of Jesus Christ of the Latter Day Saints (the LDS Church). They are microfilming as many parish registers of England as possible and extracting all the names onto a microfiche index known as the International Genealogical Index (IGI).

The IGI is arranged by county, then alphabetically by surname. Within surnames, events are arranged chronologically. For instance, all John Smiths in one county are listed together chronologically, the first baptism being at the top of the list, the last baptism, marriage or burial at the bottom. As the program is on-going, no county is one hundred percent completed, but information on some is very detailed. You may have to go through several counties. If the surname you are searching is unusual, the IGI can give you an indication of the geographic area in which to search, if not the exact location.

To find the LDS Library nearest you, write to the Genealogical Library, 54 E. South Temple Street, Salt Lake City, UT 84111.

Each branch library can arrange to borrow microfilm from Salt Lake City for you at a cost of $2.50 for two weeks' loan. Amongst the material available to help you locate your ancestors' parish you will find:

-Boyd's Marriage Index: arranged by county and then parish. Percival Boyd attempted to build a complete index of marriages from 1536-1837; of course, he only partially succeeded, but his work can benefit you, particularly if you are researching an unusual name.

-indexes of the births, marriages and deaths registered since 1837. These are the same ones you can consult in London (see Chapter 5), but the series is not yet complete. (You will have to get the actual certificates from London.)

-British genealogies: check if yours has already been researched; it could cut down your work enormously.

-parish registers: not all, but many.

-the British Censuses, 1841-1881. (See Chapter 5.)

You can readily see that much of your research can be done on this side of the Atlantic. What a blessing this is; it means you can use your time more fruitfully in England, consulting sources that cannot be found in the United States.

Keeping Your Records In Order

Everyone has his or her own system of filing research and it is important that you have one, too. Don't just throw your notes in a folder or box hoping one day to create order out of mayhem. Devise a plan and stick with it. Here is mine: I guarantee it works for me.

For each surname I have a large brown envelope into which go all my notes. Each book or record cunsulted on that name is recorded on a piece of notepaper with the surname in the upper right hand corner and the place/ call number/ date in the left margin. These are also recorded on a Research Index (see Fig. 1C), even if the search was fruitless, and the index pages are numbered. Any correspondence is also kept in order and recorded on a Correspondence Index.

All family group sheets and pedigree charts are in a blue folder, in alphabetical order by head of household. Spare forms are also kept in here. This is really the master index to your complete research. You should be able to quite easily look up details of any individual and the research which led you to him.

Fig. 1C RESEARCH INDEX

Surname of interest: Page:
Name and address of researcher:

Record repository	Call #	Description of source	Results	File #

OUTLINE OF MAIN EVENTS IN BRITISH HISTORY

	Political	Social/Economic
1066	Norman conquest Emergence of Britain as a nation	Feudal system Castle building
1170-1200	The Crusades	Era of monasteries
1215	Magna Carta signed	Courts established
1422	Accession of Henry VI Wars of the Roses	Breakdown of civil government
1485	Accession of Henry VII	Beginning of state control End of feudal system
1536	Reformation of the Church Beginning of parish registers	First industrial revolution Breakdown of medieval society Emergence of a middle class Grammar schools founded
1641-1649	Civil War	
1650-1660	Inter-regnum – the Commonwealth of Oliver Cromwell	Church of England reasserts its dominance over rising non-conformists Middle-class becomes a permanent part of society Many migrate to U.S.
1714	Accession of George I	
1750		Beginning of the Agricultural & Industrial Revolutions Mass population movements to industrial cities
1776-1783	War of American Independence	
1793-1815	Napoleonic Wars Supremacy of British Navy	
1837	Accession of Queen Victoria Beginning of civil registration	Era of industrial slums Railways begin service Popular education begun by churches
1854-1856	Crimean War	
1870	Beginning of a large wave of working class migration to U.S. (to 1900)	State elementary education begun
1901	Death of Queen Victoria Boer War	
1914-1918	World War I	Many social changes; e.g., women working, gradual disappearance of servant class

Geography Of England

It is my common experience that few Americans know the location of any English city except London - many seem to equate London and England as one and the same! Do not let this be you!

Firstly, familiarize yourself with the counties. In 1974, the boundaries were changed - some counties ceased to exist and new ones were created. (See Maps 1d & 1e.) You will need to know if the counties in which you are interested were affected, because each county has a record office (archives), and it would be wasteful of time and money to go to the wrong one.

You will need a more detailed map for travel in England. A modern road atlas, such as the AA Road Atlas of Great Britain, available through the British Tourist Authority, is a good start. You may also want to acquire Frank Smith's Genealogical Gazeteer of England (1977), which gives information on extinct chapelries, villages, and parishes as well as thriving ones.

Planning Research Objectives In England

A research trip will be costly and probably of a relatively short duration - there will not be time to waste on wild goose chases. Therefore, the key to a successful expedition is planning.

1) Organize your completed research. Read carefully through your completed work on your English lines, with a notepad at your elbow. As you read, ideas will occur for 'solutions' to the various research 'problems': when was X born?; were Y and Z his parents?; is so, how can it be proven or disproven? For each family, construct a list of ideas to follow up. If you have a particularly sticky or dead-end problem, try to discuss it with a more experienced colleague.

2) Examine your list of ideas and determine which can be followed through in the US. Keep in mind the tools available at LDS branch libraries.

3) Exhaust all possibilities. This will pare down your list to research that cannot be done in the US, e.g.:

-parish registers not microfilmed by the Latter Day Saints program.

-parish registers searched on microfilm which you suspect may have missing pages.

-probate records.

-civil registration.

-miscellaneous records which may be in libraries or County Record Offices. (See Chapter 4 or Public Record Office Chapter 5.)

-graveyard inscriptions.

-oral interviews.

4) Lay out your research objectives in a logical order. If you need to confirm a suspicion before embarking on a second idea, plan your itinerary accordingly. (It is not always possible to do this, in which case all potentially pertinent data at the second location will have to be noted and then left to a process of elimination by subsequent findings.)

Example: At St. Peter's, Totting, you find the baptism of three John Halls, any of which might be your man. List them all, plus any other Halls, in your notes. At Bingham All Souls you discover a marriage entry that lists "John Hall, labourer of Totting, married Anne Bone, spinster, of this parish" with the groom's father, Zebedee, witnessing with his mark. You can now single out the correct John from your notes at Totting.

5) Write to all the locations (churches, libraries, and record offices) which you plan to visit and make an appointment. Try to describe, as exactly as possible, the records you wish to consult. The purpose of this is two-fold: firstly, to find out if that source actually holds the records you believe it to; secondly, to warn the custodian well in advance so he can have the records ready for you.

THE ENGLISH COUNTIES PRIOR
TO 1974

THE ENGLISH COUNTIES
SINCE 1974

Northumberland

Tyne & Wear

Cumbria

Durham

Cleveland

Isle of Man

North Yorkshire

Humberside

Lancashire

West Yorkshire

Merseyside

Greater Manchester

South Yorkshire

Lincolnshire

Cheshire

Derby

Nottingham

WALES

Stafford

Salop (Shropshire)

West Midlands

Leicester

Norfolk

Hereford & Worcester

Warwick

Northampton

Cambridge

Suffolk

Bedford

Hertford

Essex

Gloucester

Oxford

Buckingham

Greater London

Avon

Wiltshire

Berkshire

Surrey

Kent

Somerset

Hampshire

West Sussex

East Sussex

Devon

Dorset

Isle of Wight

Cornwall

In writing to parishes, give two alternate dates and enclose two International Reply Coupons (available at all U.S. Post Offices) for reply. (See sample letter below.) Names and addresses of Church of England priests can be found in Crockford's Clerical Directory. Most LDS branch libraries hold a copy.

Sample Letter:

> 1234 Washington Street
> Lincoln, Ohio 12345
> U.S.A.

Rev. O. B. Smith
The Rectory
Middle Snoring
Gloucestershire, GL37NX
England   1 January 1985

Dear Rev. Smith,
 I am conducting research into my family's ancestry and would like an appointment to read the baptismal registers of Middle Snoring from 1752 to 1812, and the burials from 1806 to 1857. Two possible dates are July 16th and 17th, whichever is most convenient to you. I am enclosing two International Reply Coupons for your use.

> Yours, etc.

Record offices only need one date option when you write for an appointment, but many have limited amounts of seating and you may need to have a table or microfilm reader reserved. In addition, the archivist may be able to suggest alternative records to consult, so a brief outline of your research goals would not come amiss. (Don't be too verbose, however, as archivists are already overburdened.) Addresses of County Record Offices can be found in Appendix A.

Send your letters air-mail. Surface mail takes six to eight weeks.

General Preparations For The Visit

Your first major decision is whether to engage a travel agent to plan and book your itinerary for you, or to do it yourself. If you have never travelled abroad before, you may feel strongly tempted to visit a travel agent, discuss your hopes and plans, and sit back, confident that your vacation is in the lap of a professional. There are, however, several considerations to be made.

Make sure that the travel agent you engage is a reputable professional. Personal recommendation by close acquaintances is probably your strongest guide, though an agent's membership in a travel agency association such as the American Society of Travel Agents, or the Association of Retail Travel Agents, is also a good plus. I hope you never experience the same frustration I had when booked on a non-existant flight to London. The travel agent had failed to relay to me a change of date, causing a 24 hour delay and the necessity of changing flights. Needless to say, I have never since engaged that particular agency!

Be aware, too, that if an agent plans and books a complete itinerary for you (as opposed to merely booking a flight), you will be charged for their professional services, including such items as cablegrams to hotels. You are paying for the agent's expertise and knowledge of the travel scene of the country you are visiting.

Additionally, most smaller European hotels, unlike large American hotel chains, do not pay travel agents a commission and, of course, do not have sales representatives in the United States. Travel agents, quite naturally, will book you into the more expensive 'name' hotels - comfortable, to be sure, but tiringly monotonous the world over. If you do not want this type of vacation, plan your own itinerary.

Self-planning will mean doing a lot of homework, especially in booking your own accommodation. Airfares can be quite a jungle, too. (Even agents cannot keep up with the daily round of gimmicks being meted out be airlines!) A self-planner can feel a sense of achievement and control of his or her time, while saving money on an agent's commission and hotel bills. The following section is therefore dedicated to the self-planner.

1) Airline Reservations. When planning the season for your vacation, bear in mind these points:

-cheapest months on scheduled carriers are October through March (except Christmas) but you are less likely to find a charter flight at that time of year.

-charter flights are usually considerably cheaper than regular or discount coach tickets. Companies will offer a discount incentive to book early, for example, before mid-April.

-regular carriers have hit back with APEX fares; seats must be purchased at least 21 days in advance and you must stay at least 7 days.

-'no-frills' airlines are now operating out of more and more cities. Tickets are one-way and, unless you live on the East Coast, will probably involve at least one stop-over. Fares are lower than those for charter flights, but you need a flexible schedule.

-standby fares are offered by the major airlines to compete with the 'no-frills' brigade. Standbys are cheaper than APEX and the voucher can be purchased in advance, but you cannot be sure of a reservation until the day of the flight. Summer season is therefore a less likely time to have standby seats left, as are Christmas and to a lesser extent Easter. To find out if there are seats available you may call the airline you have selected on their toll-free number, rather than camp out at the airport. It is really an efficient system and quite painless as long as your schedule has some flexibility.

2) Booking Accomodations. The prospective traveller can be dazzled by the variety of alternatives available. Go over this section carefully before deciding what you want to do.

-'name' hotels exist in Britain and can be booked through the regular reservations system here in the US. Several disadvantages must be mentioned, however. Firstly, to be profitable the large chain hotels are usually situated in a metropolitan area such as London, Birmingham or Glasgow; okay for the conventional tourist but not for the genealogist who wishes to investigate the wilds of Norfolk! Secondly, chain hotels are impersonal and do not reflect local color to such a degree as you might want. Thirdly, they are expensive.

-'go-as-you-please tours' are arranged by companies such as Thompson's or British Airways. You select the category of hotel you want and are supplied with vouchers good for a range of hotels up and down the country (usually British 'chains' such as Embassy or Trust House Forte). These are usually less expensive than 'name' hotels, and just as comfortable with private bath and TV in each room. Many are converted from older mansions or homes and have great charm. You are unlikely to find one in an out-of-the-way spot but perhaps you might compromise a little and rent a car out, an option which will be discussed in a later section.

-private hotels and guest houses range in size from a manor house down to a terraced city dwelling. Some have private baths, many do not. Smaller guest houses are usually private homes which offer 'bed and breakfast' in the tourist season. Locally they are known as b & b's.

How can you, a foreigner, distinguish the good from the bad? Write to the regional tourist board of the area in which you are planning to stay (see Appendix C) and ask for a list of approved hotels and guesthouses (establishments which are inspected regularly and meet official guidelines). The list also grades the type of accommodation from de-luxe down to good, and will give the price-range and any facilities such as a bar, TV Lounge, or babysitting service.

You will also find on the list an in-
triguing variety of places offering b &
b - from farmhouses to castles. One of
my most enjoyable visits was to Durham,
where I had a room in the castle's keep:
walls fifteen feet thick, breakfast and
a gourmet evening meal in the medieval
great hall and all a stone's throw from
the cathedral and city center.

3) How to book accomodations in advance:

-select several places in the same area,
 in case your first choice is booked.

-write to the proprietor, specifying
 your dates, the number of people in
 your party, and how many rooms you will
 need. Enclose a deposit to the value
 of the first nights' accommodation.
 This should be a cashier's check for
 the correct number of dollars plus
 three extra to cover bank conversion in
 England.

Summary

At least one year prior to your trip:

-check over your research to date. Plan
 out carefully the research that needs
 to be done and follow through as much
 as possible in the United States.   An
 outline of the genealogical research
 process:

        Collect oral evidence
                 ↓
        Collect family documents
                 ↓
          Evaluate contents
            ↙   ↘
File in surname   Seek supporting
   folder   primary evidence
          ↖   ↙
          Evaluate contents
                 ↓
Place conclusions on pedigree charts and
        family group sheets
                 ↓
        Establish new goals

-make an outline of your research plans
 in England and plan an itinerary around
 this.

-write for appointments with record
 offices and clergy.

-write to Regional Tourists Boards for
 hotel lists and make reservations.

-keep a close check on the airfare situation. Decide which type of fare best
 suits your needs and book accordingly.

Further Reading

The Genealogical Helper. Logan, Utah:
Everton. (Bi-monthly magazine.)

Greenwood, Val D. The Researcher's
Guide To American Genealogy, Baltimore
MD; Genealogical Publishing Co., 1973.

Smith, Frank and David Gardner. Genealogical Research In England And Wales.
(3 vols.) Salt Lake City, Utah: Bookcraft, 1959, 1964, 1976.
Westin, Jean Eddy. Finding Your Roots.
New York: Ballantine, 1977.

Wright, Norman Edgar. Building An Amer-
ican Pedigree: A Study In Genealogy.
Provo, Utah; Brigham Young University
Press, 1974.

CHAPTER 2

WHAT TO TAKE TO ENGLAND

This chapter is designed as a checklist for the reader's convenience. Samples of charts and forms may be copied.

Genealogical Supplies

Pedigree charts
Family group sheets
Research index forms
Will forms
Census forms, 1841-1881 (Chart 1)
Birth, marriage, death registration
  search forms (Chart 2)
Marriage registration search records
  (Chart 3)
Baptismal register - search records
  (Chart 4)
Records of previous relevant research
An adjustable focus 35mm camera
Black and white film (print or
  transparency)
Colour film
Pencils with erasers
Pencil sharpener
Legal pads

Clothing & Accessories

All year round

  Sturdy walking shoes
  Light plastic foldaway raincoat
  Light jackets or cardigans
  Old jeans
  Old shirt or sweater
  Knee-high rainboots or slipovers
  Umbrella

Winter

  Heavy coat (waterproof)
  Warm or thermal underwear
  Gloves
  Scarf
  Wolly hat
  Heavy wool sweaters
  Heavyweight pants
  Snow-type boots

Spring and Autumn

  Lighter sweaters
  Gloves
  Headscarf or cap
  Light raincoat
  Shoes

Summer

  Dresses
  Cotton skirts
  Short-sleeved blouses/shirts
  Light-weight pants
  Sandals
  Shoes

Personal Items

Passport
International Driver's License
  (available from American Automobile
  Association)
Britrail pass issued by British Rail
  (see Chapter 3)
Coach Pass

Personal Items (continued)

Credit cards: Visa, Mastercard, American
 Express, Diner's Club
Travelers checks in pounds sterling
Maps: road map, small scale maps
Itinerary
List of addresses of accommodations
List of appointments booked, with
 addresses
Flight tickets

Note About Maps

Good road maps of Great Britain are available in most bookstores at a reasonable price, but they do tend to become outdated estremely quickly. For the genealogist, small-scale maps of areas of interest (Ordnance Survey Maps) are available from Her Majesty's Stationary Office, 49 High Holborn, London WC1V 6HB. These maps show small details such as farmhouses and trails.

A PRACTICAL GUIDE FOR THE GENEALOGIST IN ENGLAND

Chart 1   18__ CENSUS FOR ENGLAND

Parish or township _____   Ecclesiastical district _____

City/Borough _____   Town/Village _____

Number	Address	Name & Surname	Relationship to head of household*	Condition*	Age# M	F	Rank, Profession or Occupation	Place of birth

*not included on 1841 Census
#rounded to nearest five years in 1841

Chart 2   10-YEAR BIRTH/MARRIAGE/DEATH RECORD SEARCH FORM

(circle appropriate record)

Name and address of researcher:
Date of research:

Name being researched:
Date of event (if known):

Instructions: Check space if quarter searched unsuccessfully.   Fill in details of
              district, and volume and page number of any possibilities.

Year	First Quarter	Second Quarter	Third Quarter	Fourth Quarter

Chart 3   MARRIAGES - RECORD OF SEARCHES

Name(s) being researched:
Date of search:
Parish searched:
Date of registers searched:
Name & address of researcher:

Date	Groom's name & status	Age	Bride's name & status	Age	Groom's parent(s) or witness	Bride's parent(s) or witness

Chart 4 BAPTISMAL REGISTERS - SEARCH RECORD

Surname(s) searched:
Parish searched:
Dates searched:
Name & address of researcher:
Date of search:

Candidates's name	Parent(s)	Date of baptism	Remarks

CHAPTER 3

COPING IN ENGLAND

Flights to England from the US are at least five hours' duration and can be as many as twelve from the West Coast. They are usually overnight, so it is advisable to sleep en route to avoid the worst excesses of jet-lag. Eat a good meal beforehand and settle down as soon as you are air-bound, asking the stewardess not to disturb you. Avoid alcoholic beverages. After a good sleep, drink juice or milk, eat breakfast, and exercise your limbs.

Most flights to London land at Heathrow, west of the capital, or at Gatwick, to the south. As soon as the descent begins, notice the rich green and yellow tapestry of fields interlaced, perhaps, with the silver ribbon of a narrow river; houses will seem squashed together. Britain is a tiny island compared to North America and space is highly prized, yet this also means that nowhere is far away. A train trip from London to York takes less than four hours. Birmingham to London is only one hour by commuter plane, 1 1/2 hours by train.

At the airport, go first through immigration control (which means very long lines for foreigners); then, after collecting you luggage, negotiate customs control. Britain has instituted a two-channel system. If you have nothing to declare, go through the green channel. Only spot-checks are made here. If you do have duty to pay, go to the red channel. Officers will be waiting to tell you how much you owe. Having charted the appropriate course through customs, you will now push your trolley of luggage into Britain.

Private Transport

Through your travel-agent in the US, you may arrange to hire a car for the period you are in England. The major firms have desks at all airports as well as throughout the country. This gives the traveler freedom from time-tables, freedom to roam at will the more rural areas, freedom from annoyances such as rail-strikes. There is a wide range of models offered, many of which will be much smaller than American cars, so consider the need for a luggage rack.

As car-hire is expensive, and gasoline (petrol) is more than twice the American price, choose energy-efficient models, a Mini-Metro or Ford Escort, for example.

Some points to remember when driving in England:

-drive on the left.

-speed limits are higher than in the US and the flow of traffic, even in towns, is more hectic.

-motorways have the designation M-; for example, the M1 runs from London northwards. These roads are equivalent to American expressways. (Speed limit: 70mph)

-a roundabout is used at crossroads very often. Be prepared to halt at the edge and merge into a gap in the traffic. Signal left one exit before your intended exit. Roundabouts are not difficult to negotiate after you have tried a few.

-you may never turn right on a red light.

-after a red light, you will see a red and amber combination before green appears. This tells you to prepare to go.

-all road signs are now European and mostly self-explanatory. A full list is given in "The Highway Code", an inexpensive booklet available from Her Majesty's Stationery Office.

-front seat passengers must use seat belts.

Public Transport

Public transport is alive and well in Britain. The national railway network (British Rail) is very extensive and buses serve even remote areas at least once a week.

Britrail passes for 7, 14, 21, and 28 days may be purchased in the US through a travel agent. The pass is activated by being stamped at a ticket office on its first day of use, and can be used to go anywhere in Britain within the speci- fied period. It is a bargain when compared to purchasing separate tickets for each journey.

British Rail uses the twenty-four-hour clock in its timetables, as do bus com- panies. Trains are fast, comfortable and generally reliable, though the food is a national joke. Porters are avail- able at all stations and should be tip- ped. All but very small stations have a buffet bar and waiting rooms.

The roadway rival to British Rail is the National Express Coach company. They run services to places often unserved by rail. A coach (the American bus), seats about 50 people and is very comfortable; a few have lavatories in the rear and some have TV's and hostesses. The major advantages are cheapness and broad scope of destinations. The disadvantages are longer journeys and poor organization at coach stations, especially Victoria in London. There is a tourist pass scheme similar to British Rail's, but it is much cheaper and does not have to be used on consecutive days; i.e., you can use up a seven-day pass over a calender month. This represents an advantage to the traveler who wants to stay several days at various points.

Bus companies provide local, short- distance service in cities, towns, and country areas. You may have to pay the driver as you enter or a conductor will come and collect fares. State your destination clearly. Busses are often unpunctual so be patient.

The London Underground deserves a section to itself. London is the only city in Britain with a subway system, but it is very extensive and for the first-time tourist, the most efficient mode of transport. There are nine lines or routes, covering much of metropolitan London. The Victoria and Jubilee lines, the most modern, are also the most clean and efficient. Some of the older lines, patricularly the Northern, are dark and dirty, but travel is pleasant and safe from vandals. Beware of pickpockets, however - some things haven't changed since Dicken's time! Buy a ticket for your destination (you can choose your own route as long as you do not leave through a station); tickets are singles, returns (round-trip) are not sold. There are rows of ticket machines at most stations, but you need the correct change for these. Ticket offices are also open, if you do not have correct change.

Eating Out

In Britain eating out is not a pastime as it is in the US and amongst families is usually reserved for very special occasions. You will not find the for- midable array of fast-food places in every nook and cranny. Yes, McDonald's has infiltrated the conurbations but Britain has fare of its own to offer the discriminating visitor. I will survey the main types of eatery, from inexpensive upwards.

1) Fish and chips shops are open lunch times and evenings. Watch for the sign "frying times" on the door or window. Fish and chips (roughly equivalent but far superior to french fries) are no longer the cheap meal they once were, but still a great British favorite, and quite reasonable. The shop-girl will surely mutter, "Salt or vinegar?" so be prepared to answer yes or no, according to whether you want your chips doused or not. Other types of food such as cornish pasties, meat pies, and peas may also be available.

2) Cafes are friendly, homelike places, offering tea, coffee, plain meals, and desserts at a very reasonable price. They are often family run, but can be found in department stores where they are called cafeterias and are self-service. Cafes in bus or coach stations are not recommended, often being dirty and the food inedible.

3) Pubs are open only at lunch-times and evenings, but pub fare has an excellent reputation. The menu is usually limited to cold sandwiches, pasties, pies, or shrimp or chicken 'in a basket'; i.e., with chips. At lunch-time the Ploughman's Lunch is a must: home-made bread, fresh cheese, pickled onions, washed down with a half-pint of ale. Many pubs are in historic inns and a convivial atmosphere is almost guaranteed.

4) Restaurants are much the same as in the US, though a town may have only one or two. Traveler's checks and credit cards are accepted. Do not expect a salad with dinner. Dishes are not described on menus but you may ask the waiter about ingredients. Some food terms are included in Appendix E.

Manners and Customs

Much emphasis is placed upon common courtesies in England - liberal use of "please" and "thank you" is much appreciated. Queuing (lining up with infinite patience) is the national pastime at bus stops, railway stations, shops, theatres - in fact, anywhere two or more are gathered. Queue-jumping must never be practiced.

Tea drinking is not merely a way of slaking one's thirst, it is the social communion of England. If you are asked to join someone for a cup of tea, try, if at all possible, to accept the offer. Britons take milk (not cream) and possibly sugar and you will be asked your preferences.

The British policeman, or 'bobby', the national symbol of integrity and helpfulness, can still be seen on foot-patrol. He is usually very good at directions, and is addressed as 'constable' (unless three stripes indicate he is a sergeant).

Many terms used in Britain will be alien even to addicts of Masterpiece Theater. Turn to Appendix E for an English/American vocabulary list.

Climate

England is predominantly a cool, damp country, hence the ubiquitous umbrella. Showers, even heavy ones, are frequent. 'Sunny periods' and 'periods of rain' are the British meteorologists' favorite phrases.

Winters bring some fog in low lying areas near water, but do not expect the pea-soupers of Victorian London. Frost is more common than snow except in the North, and temperatures rarely fall below 28 degrees Fahreneit. A cold piercing rain is common, often with high winds.

Summers are pleasantly warm, around 65-70 degrees Fahreneit, with rain showers, and there is no need for air-conditioning. Sightseeing is enjoyable.

Spring and autumn are unpredictable seasons; it is very hard to know what to

expect. Probably it is best to be prepared for the worst! Remember Keats
wrote of autumn as "season of mists and
mellow fruitfulness."

Electrical Gadgets

Britain's electricity supply runs on 220
volts, double that of the US, so any
electrical appliances you take to England will require an adaptor. It may be
more worthwhile to use disposable razors
and see a hairdresser once a week.

Currency

The units of currency are one hundred
pennies (p) to one pound (₤). Coins are
1p, 2p, 5p, 10p, 20p, 50p, & ₤1. Notes
(bills) are ₤5, ₤10, ₤20. ₤1 coins are
extremely unpopular and easily confused
with the 10p coin. Visa is widely
accepted, followed by American Express.
Mastercard and Diner's Club are less
well-known.

Telephones

The telephone system is a nationwide
company. When dialing an in-town call,
it is not necessary to dial the town
code. Out-of- town calls will require
the town code. International calls can
be dialed direct anywhere in Britain and
require use of the country code.

CHAPTER 4

RECORD OFFICES AND LIBRARIES

County councils were created by an Act of Parliament in 1889 and very soon afterwards, several councils began to take an active interest in the ancient documents within their jurisdiction. Bedfordshire created the first county office in the 1920's and has been followed by all other counties and major cities. Many incorporate the Diocesan Record Office.

Facilities for the researcher vary enormously. The number of staff can range from two to twenty, including professional archivists as well as technical and clerical staff. Space is often severely limited.

The Jurisdiction Of Record Offices

Each county or city record office will vary greatly in its accessions, and it is therefore essential to write beforehand to determine that they have what you need. Here is a basic checklist of probable types of records:

County records: courts, shire
Local Board of Health
Boards of Guardians
School managers and boards
Borough records
Censuses (county only-microfilm)
Probate
Non-conformist or R C registers
Bishops' Transcripts (B.T.'s)
Marriage licenses
Meeting-house certificates
Recusancy Records
Estate Records

Family archives - diaries, letters, journals
Printed and pictorial records
Parish records (see Chapter 6)

A reminder about note-keeping: use only pencils in record offices. Be meticulous and accurate. Chart all searchs on Research Index forms.

Libraries

Local libraries may be an unexpected source of information. Many have acquired microfilm copies of the censuses for their area and may have a good collection of local newspapers. Most will have the Victoria County History and possibly other local histories, genealogies, and maps. A list of larger libraries with major collections is incorporated into Appendix A, but it was not feasible to include all libraries. Do be aware of their potential, however.

The Public Record Office

Ruskin Avenue
Richmond, Surrey TW9 4DV
Telephone: 01 876 3444

Open 9:30 am - 5:00 pm, Monday through Friday. Closed the first two weeks of October.

The Public Record Office has three repositories at present: Kew, Chancery Lane, and Portugal Street, London. Kew is by far the most valuable for genealogists in the variety of sources it offers for research, but the first-time visitor cannot expect to tap the P.R.O's resources to the full. It takes many visits and much experience to gain the most from each visit. That said, do not be discouraged - do your homework beforehand, come prepared with specific research objectives, but be flexible so you can follow up on new clues.

To consult public records you must obtain a reader's ticket in advance by writing to the above address. There is no charge for the ticket. When writing, take the opportunity to double-check that the records you wish to consult are at Kew; re-organistations do take place from time to time and you do not want to find yourself twenty-five miles from the correct repository! (Travel across London can be painfully slow and waste precious hours.)

Many of the records come from governmental agencies, such as the War Office, the Admiralty, the Foreign Office, and the Treasury. The records remain classified according to their department of origin and abbreviations are used. Some of the main abbreviations you will meet are:

ADM - Admiralty
BT - Board of Trade
CO - Colonial Office
E   - Exchequer
FO - Foreign Office
HO - Home Office
PC - Privy Council
T   - Treasury
WO - War Office
SP - State Paper Office
PMG - Paymaster General's Office
RG - General Register Office

For example, a naval record might be designated ADM 100, an army record WO 312.

Following are the main types of records in the P.R.O.:

a) Nonconformist (or non-parochial) church registers. The P.R.O. has about 9,000 registers from churches other than the established Anglican church. They are mainly Protestant and only a few pre-date the eighteenth century. Early eighteenth century registers recorded baptisms, marriages and burials, but after 1754 all marriages had to be solemnised in the Church of England, and so will not show in the nonconformist registers.

There are also a few Roman Catholic registers in the P.R.O., mainly from the northern counties of England. In general, registers remain with the priest or diocese. If you have difficulty in locating a particular Catholic parish register, write to the Catholic Central Library, 41 Francis Street, London SW1P 1DN; or to the Catholic Record Society, c/o Miss R Rendal, Flat 5, Lennox Gardens, London SW1X 0BQ.

b) Wills prior to 1858. Before 1858 the proving or 'probate' of wills was purely an ecclesiastical matter and occurred in the Prerogative Court of the Province (York of Canterbury), or in the diocesan court. The P.R.O. has wills proved in the Prerogative Court of Canterbury (abbreviated to P.C.C.) from 1384 to 1858. Don't get too excited though - these are wills of persons of substantial means and the chances that you ancestor was such a person are slim. If the surname you are researching is uncommon, however, it would certainly be worth searching the indexes described below. You may also hold the conviction that your ancestor was a notable and this is a way to document that idea.

Indexes To Wills:

-Camp, A.J. P.C.C. Will Index, 1750-1800. Volume 1: Surnames A-Bh, Volume 2: Surnames Bi-Ce. Completion of this project will obviously take many decades, but it is sorely needed to update the project of the British Record Society.

-Prerogative Court of Canterbury Wills (British Record Society). Twelve volumes spanning 1384 to 1700. Each volume covers the wills for a specific period and indexes the deceased's names alphabetically. Many large libraries and genealogical collections hold this set.

-Card Index to P.C.C. Wills, 1721-25: held by the Society of Genealogists.

When using these indexes, be careful to copy the full name of the deceased, date of death or probate, and refernce number of the will.

Reading wills is not an easy task, especially those prior to the nineteenth century. See Chapter 9 for guidance in reading and interpreting these documents.

c) Tax records. Ever since Julius Caesar stood on England's shore and uttered the famous dictum "Veni, vidi, vici", the English people have been subjected to an ever-increasing tide of taxation. Fortunately for the genealogist, this means that lists have been generated for residents who might otherwise have gone unrecorded.

The Hearth Tax, imposed between 1662 and 1674, is probably the most complete and useful of the earlier taxes. It required householders to pay a tax of two shillings on each hearth in the house. Not only do we have househoulders' names but we can also infer their status according to the number of hearths. The most complete set of records is for the tax collected on March 25, 1664. Many have been indexed and printed by local groups.

The Land Tax Redemption Office Quotas and Assessments for 1798-1799 are also valuable documents. All landowners in England and Wales are listed, town by town and village by village. Sadly it remains unindexed, making a location absolutely necessary beforehand.

d) Military records. The British Army has been a regularly organised body for several hundred years. Until the mid-nineteenth century, its organization was rather looser than we now associate with that institution, but it left a mass of records for the genealogist. The Army is divided into regiments, which were often associated with a county. There are four types of regiment:

infantry - foot soldiers
cavalry - horseback soldiers
artillery - cannon-firers
engineers - constructors of bridges, roads, etc.

Each regiment consists of commissioned officers, non-commissioned officers (who have risen from the ranks) and private soldiers. Commissions were bought and sold, a practice which effectively kept them within the domain of the upper classes.

The officer classes were, perhaps inevitably, better documented than the rank and file. Look first in the Army Lists, published annually since 1754; a complete set is available at the Society of Genealogists. This will verify your ancestor's regiment(s) and career record. The P.R.O. has a regimental list of officers for the years 1702-1823 (WO 64). If there is any indication of involvement in campaigns, consult the Medal Rolls (WO 100) for details. Genealogical information can be gleaned from applications for commissions (WO 31) and widows' pensions (WO 42).

The career of the ordinary soldier is, alas, more difficult to reconstruct, and genealogical data is very limited. After 1883 discharge papers are arranged alphabetically regardless of regiment, thus easy to locate. Before that date, however, it is totally essential to know the man's regiment before consulting the War Office records, which run into the hundreds of thousands. If you think your ancestor served in a particular campaign, consult a military history to ascertain the regiments involved. One of my Irish ancestors supposedly served in the Crimea with great distinction, but so far I have been unable to locate any refernce to him. It is my only clue, though, and I continue to be guided by it. Again, if medals were awarded to the ancestor, consult the Medal Rolls (WO 100). When you have found which regiment your ancestor belonged to, you can try searching the

Regular Soldiers' Documents (WO 97) which detail soldiers' complete service record. The series runs from 1756 to 1913.

In the Naval records, officers are, again, much better documented than ratings are, and it is essential to know on which ship he served if he was in the Navy before 1853. Officer's careers have been published in the Navy Lists annually since 1814, and there are also many naval biographies such as Commissioned Sea Officers of the Royal Navy, 1660-1815 (London, 1954). Primary sources such as the Captains Logs (ADM 51) may then be searched.

Unless his ship is known, a rating is very difficult to locate. Medal Rolls (ADM 171) can be of help. The Ship's Musters (ADM 36-39) give a great detail about the ratings' naval careers and even date and place of birth in some instances. These records survive from 1667 onwards. In the absence of a muster, Ship's Pay Books can confirm the man's presence aboard ship.

The Merchant seaman record holdings of the P.R.O. relate mainly to the years 1837-1857. They include Ship's Registers (1835-1857) and some muster rolls (1747-1834). Crew lists are accessible by reference to the Registers, but be warned that the system is complex after 1845 and you may want to leave this research to a professional.

The P.R.O. does not hold Royal Air Force records. Personnel records may be released to relatives only by applying to the R.A.F. Personnel Management Centre, Easter Ave., Barnwood, Gloucester GL4 7AN.

e) Records relating to British citizens abroad. Some registers of births, marriages, and deaths abroad were kept at various embassies and are now in the records of the Foreign Office at the P.R.O. Wills of Britons dying abroad were usually proven in the Prerogative Court of Canterbury and are therefore in the P.R.O. (See above.) These are records of many British nationals, not merely civil servants of Crown employees.

Births, marriages, and deaths at sea from 1854 to1890 are among the records of the Board of Trade (BT 158). Deaths at sea of British nationals 1825-1880 are classified under BT 159, and births at sea 1875-1891 are in BT 160.

f) Emigrations records. Formal emigration lists have never been kept, but the following classes of documents might be useful to the American genealogist:

-BT 27 - Passenger Lists, 1890-1960; arranged by year and port of departure, they give the name, age, occupation and last address of the passenger.

-T 47/9-12 - Register of emigrants to America, 1773-1776, for which there is a card index. The index gives name, age, occupation, reason for leaving Britain, last address and destination.

-AO 12 - American Loyalists' Claims 1776-1831

-AO 13 - American Loyalists' Claims 1780-1835

g) Deeds. There are thousands of deeds in the Public Record Office but unfortunately there is no index to the majority of them. They are arranged in chronological order by the date of filing and there is a notation of the county in the margin. You may wish to hire a professional researcher if you are fairly confident that a deed exists and do not have the time to search on your own.

Two considerations need to be kept in mind. Firstly, that land and property ownership has until this century been the exclusive preserve of a very small class of English society. The chances that your ancestor held property are quite limited. Secondly, until the nineteenth century, there was no legal requirement to keep deeds or to record transfer of ownership. Most people held land by copyhold, a form of tenure now abolished, and transfers were recorded on the court roll of the manor. Most court rolls are held by the county record offices and many have been printed by archaeological societies.

h) Census returns. See Chapter 5.

i) Apprenticeship records.   See Chapter 6.

What Not To Expect At The P.R.O. (Kew)

Formal genealogies
Anglican parish registers
Birth, marriage or death records
Wills after 1858
Records of soldiers serving in the Boer
  War, World Wars I or II.

Fig 4:1 Public Record Office, Kew

BRENTFORD

Kew Bridge

CHISWICK

River Thames

Kew Green

PUBLIC RECORD OFFICE

KEW RD.

FOREST RD.

DISTRICT LINE

MORTLAKE

RUSKIN AVE.

DEFOE AVE.

Royal Botanic Gardens

LEYBORNE PK.

BURLINGTON AV.

BEECHWOOD AV.

ROAD

STATION APPROACH

WEST PARK RD.

HIGH PARK RD.

KEW GARDENS STATION

KEW ROAD

SANDYCOMBE RD.

NORTH ROAD

NORTH SHEEN

n

¼ mile

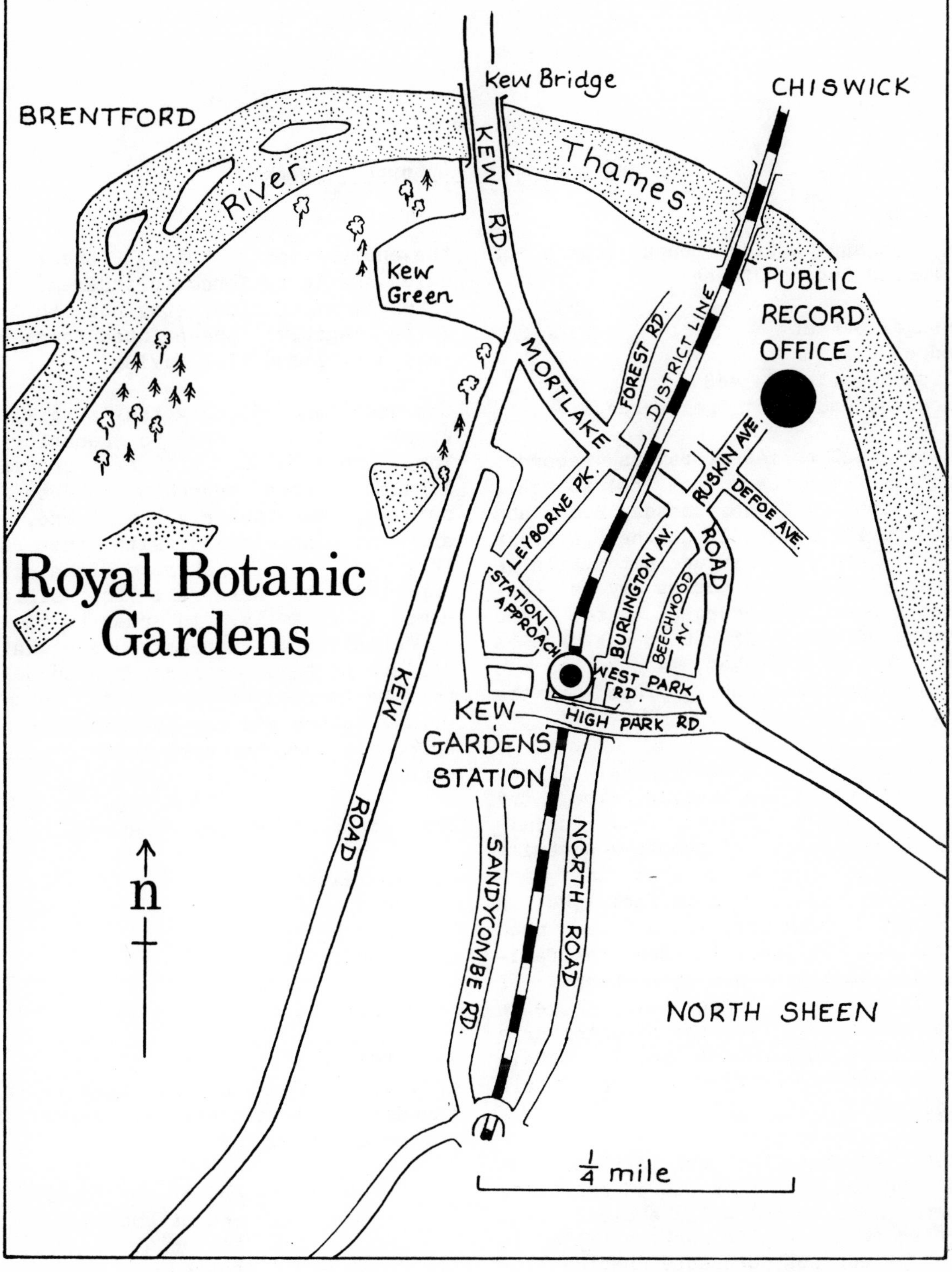

CHAPTER 5

OTHER LONDON RECORD REPOSITORIES

Land Registry Office (Census branch of the Public Record Office)

Portugal Street
London WC2A 1LR
Telephone: 01-405-3488
Hours: 9:30am to 5:30pm weekdays

The original copies of census records, taken every ten years from 1841 to 1881, are housed with the Domesday Book and other fragile materials at the P.R.O. in Chancery Lane. They are not available for use. Microfilm copies may be consulted, free of charge, at the Land Registry Office. If you do not have a P.R.O. reader's ticket, a day-pass can be obtained without a fuss at the entrance.

Be warned: this is a busy place! If you cannot arrive at the opening time, try the lunch hour. You may feel intimidated by the hoards of people who really look as if they know what they are doing, but you will soon feel like an old hand. Come prepared with as much information as possible about the families for whom you are searching. If they lived in a large town, have a street address. (Was the ancestor or a sibling born in a census year? Obtain the birth certificate for their residence.)

The Office has its own system for obtaining the microfilm needed and large posters hung on the walls explain what you need to do: a slip must be filled in with the correct reference numbers for the enumeration district, street, etc., which are to be found in indexes. Despite lack of time, try not to rush. Write legibly: pre-printed forms prove very useful and time saving.

Censuses are probably the single most vital public record to genealogists. They should be used with care and intelligence. When searching an area for a surname, particularly a rare one, note all the individuals with that name. They may tie in later. Often it is important to have all the siblings' names in a family, in order to identify it definitely. Perhaps you see what you believe to be an enumerator's error; do not be tempted to correct it automatically. Later you may not remember whose error it was, or even that it was an error.

Some notes on British censuses:

Dates Taken:
  7 June 1841
30 March 1851
  8 April 1861
  3 April 1871
  4 April 1881

The 1841 census was the first, not destroyed, to record names. Ages in it are rounded to the nearest five years. Some abbreviations used:

/   end of one family
//   end of house
Y/N Yes or No
N.K. Not Known

1841 census abbreviations (continued)

Ind. Independent means
J. Journeyman
F.W.K. Framework knitter
F.S./M.S. Female or male servant
Agr. or Ag. Lab. Agricultural Labourer

The 1851 & later censuses give:
 actual age
 place of birth
 relationship to head of household
 marital status

St. Catherine's House (birth & marriage certificates)

10 Kingsway
London WC2B 6JP
Telephone: 01-242-0262
Hours: 8:30am to 4:30pm weekdays

Only the indexes of births and marriages registered since 1 July 1837, are available for public consultation. Actual certificate copies must be purchased. The indexes are located on the first floor. Early indexes are handwritten, and all the volumes are very large and heavy. Bring your own muscles. There is no place to sit, although there are reading tables between shelves.

Each year is divided into quarters. A birth or marriage registered towards the end of a quarter are often in the next quarter's entries because the registrant was allowed several weeks to complete the formality. Every quarter's entries are arranged in alphabetical order and some require more than one volume. The actual dates of birth or marriage are not given; only the registration district, volume and page number. These must be carefully copied onto order forms and taken to the clerk. The fee is four pounds and sixty pence for each certificate. It takes 48 hours to prepare one, so a return trip is necessary.

NOTE: Do not be tempted to buy the short form of the birth certificate, which is cheaper. It will contain nothing of genealogical interest.

Other indexes:

Births and deaths at sea: 1 July, 1837 to 31 December, 1874
British births abroad since 1 July, 1849
Army returns of births, marriages and deaths from 1761
Royal Air Force returns of births, marriages and deaths since 1920

Alexandra House

Kingsway, London
Hours: as St. Catherine's House

Alexandra House in recent years housed the indexes to all death registrations since 1837, as well as original certificates. The indexing system is identical to that described for St. Catherine's House; i.e., the year is divided into four quarters and names are arranged alphabetically within each quarter. Fees are five pounds per certificate.

There are plans afoot to remove the death indexes to St. Catherine's House after enlargement of the reading room facilities has been finished. As the two offices are only a few minutes' walk apart, it is not essential to be forewarned of the move, and no date has yet been announced.

Information given on English death certificates includes the following:

Date of death
Name and address of deceased
Age and occupation of deceased
Cause of death
Signature and address of informant
Date of registration

A glance will tell you that there is not much value to the genealogists, but it may be useful to clear up a case of mistaken identity, for example. Additionally, bear in mind that information on death certificates can only, at best, be secondary source material, as the primary source is dead.

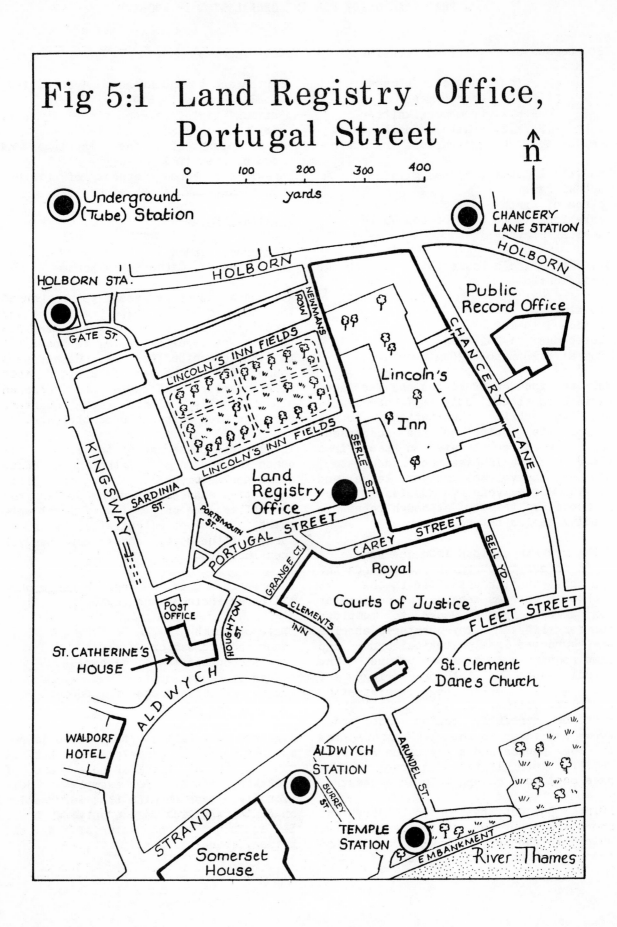

Fig 5:1 Land Registry Office, Portugal Street

n

Underground (Tube) Station

CHANCERY LANE STATION

HOLBORN STA.

HOLBORN

HOLBORN

Public Record Office

GATE ST.

NEWMAN'S ROW

LINCOLN'S INN FIELDS

Lincoln's Inn

CHANCERY LANE

KINGSWAY

LINCOLN'S INN FIELDS

SARDINIA ST.

SERLE ST.

PORTSMOUTH ST.

Land Registry Office

PORTUGAL STREET

CAREY STREET

BELL YD.

GRANGE CT.

Royal

POST OFFICE

HOUGHTON ST.

CLEMENTS INN

Courts of Justice

FLEET STREET

ST. CATHERINE'S HOUSE

St. Clement Danes Church

ALDWYCH

WALDORF HOTEL

ALDWYCH STATION

ARUNDEL ST.

STRAND

SURREY ST.

TEMPLE STATION

EMBANKMENT

River Thames

Somerset House

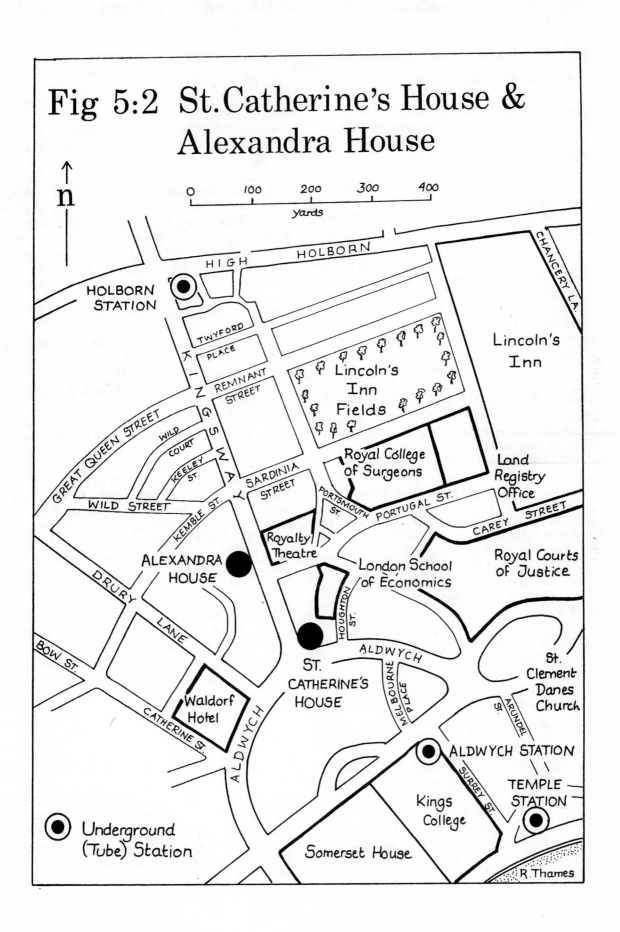

Fig 5:2 St.Catherine's House & Alexandra House

Society of Genealogists

14 Charterhouse Buildings
London, E.C. 1M 7BA
Telephone: 01-251-8799
Hours: Tuesday, Friday and Saturday –
10:00am – 6:00pm. Wednesday and
Thursday – 10:00am – 8:00pm.

Until 1984 this venerable institution
was located in a small Victorian house
near Earls' Court, but in July 1984, re-
opened at the new and larger location.

Members of the Society may use the
library free of charge, but visitors pay
a fee as follows:

Ŀ2 for one hour
Ŀ4 for 3 1/2 hours
Ŀ6 for a day
Ŀ7 1/2 for a day and evening

Membership costs $43 for the first year,
$28 thereafter annually, but is not
automatic on application. Each appli-
cant is scrutinized by the Society
before being admitted.

A checklist of records at the Society:

Printed and manuscript parish register
  transcripts
Directories
Military and Naval lists
Wills and marriage licenses
Times (of London) obituaries
Boyd's Marriage Index
Printed family histories
London 'society' periodicals
Boyd's Inhabitants of London
Pedigrees
East India Company records
Medical and professional directories
Family history magazines
Great Slip Index (800 boxes of indexed
  biographical material)
International Genealogical Index
  (appointment necessary)

The collection is a vast one and best
use of it can only come with practice
and familiarity, but do not be discon-
certed. Use what you can.

Principle Probate Registry

Somerset House
Strand, London WC2
Telephone: 01 405 7641
Hours: 10:00am to 4:30pm weekdays only.
Copies of wills can be made for 25p per
  page

All wills for the period 1858 to present
are here, fully indexed and in English
(and generally legible). If none of
your direct ancestors appears to have
left a will, try collateral branches –
valuable data may still be obtained from
them.

The British Library

a) Reading Room at the British Museum,
Great Russell Street.
Telephone: 01 363 1544
Hours: Monday thru Saturday 9:00am to
5:00pm

The Reading Room of the British Museum
is the equivalent of the US Library of
Congress. It houses virtually every
book ever published in Britain, including local histories and biographies,
perhaps even books written by your ancestor. Many, of course, are rare and
you may find a long sought-after genealogy or city directory. Make out a
list beforehand of what you hope to
locate.

It is necessary to apply for a reader's
ticket well in advance. If you are not
absolutely sure you will be visiting the
Reading Room, do not hesitate to apply
for a card anyway – better to be safe
than sorry.

b) Newspaper Library
Colindale Ave
London NW9
Telephone: 01 205 6039 or 4788

All nineteenth and twentieth century
newspapers, provincial and foreign before 1800 are housed at the Newspaper
Library. As you can imagine, the volume
of material is staggering, so it is
essential to have a specific date and
location for your search. You will fill

in a request slip and a page will bring you the papers from the stacks.

Newspapers are a very useful tool for the genealogist, capable of providing information which might otherwise have gone unrecorded. This is particularly true of obituaries. My grandmother's revealed that my grandfather had been a city councillor and she had therefore been given a civic funeral.

LDS Branch Library

64-68 Exhibition Road
London SW 2
Telephone: 01-589-8561

Located conveniently near the South Kensington underground station, the LDS Library has the microfiche I.G.I., standard English genealogical reference books, and microfilm of many parish registers.

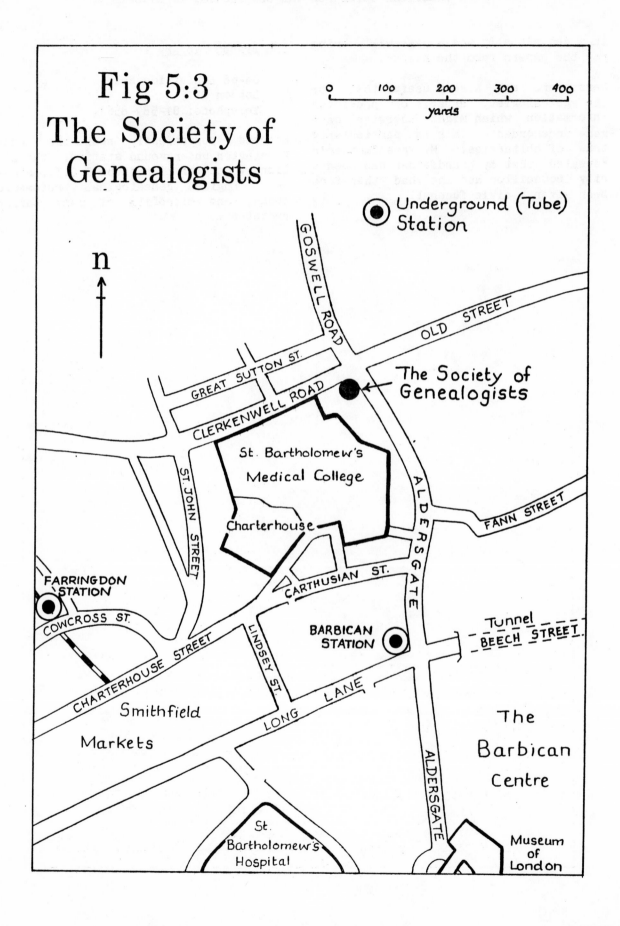

Fig 5:3
The Society of
Genealogists

Fig 5:4 Somerset House Principal Probate Registry

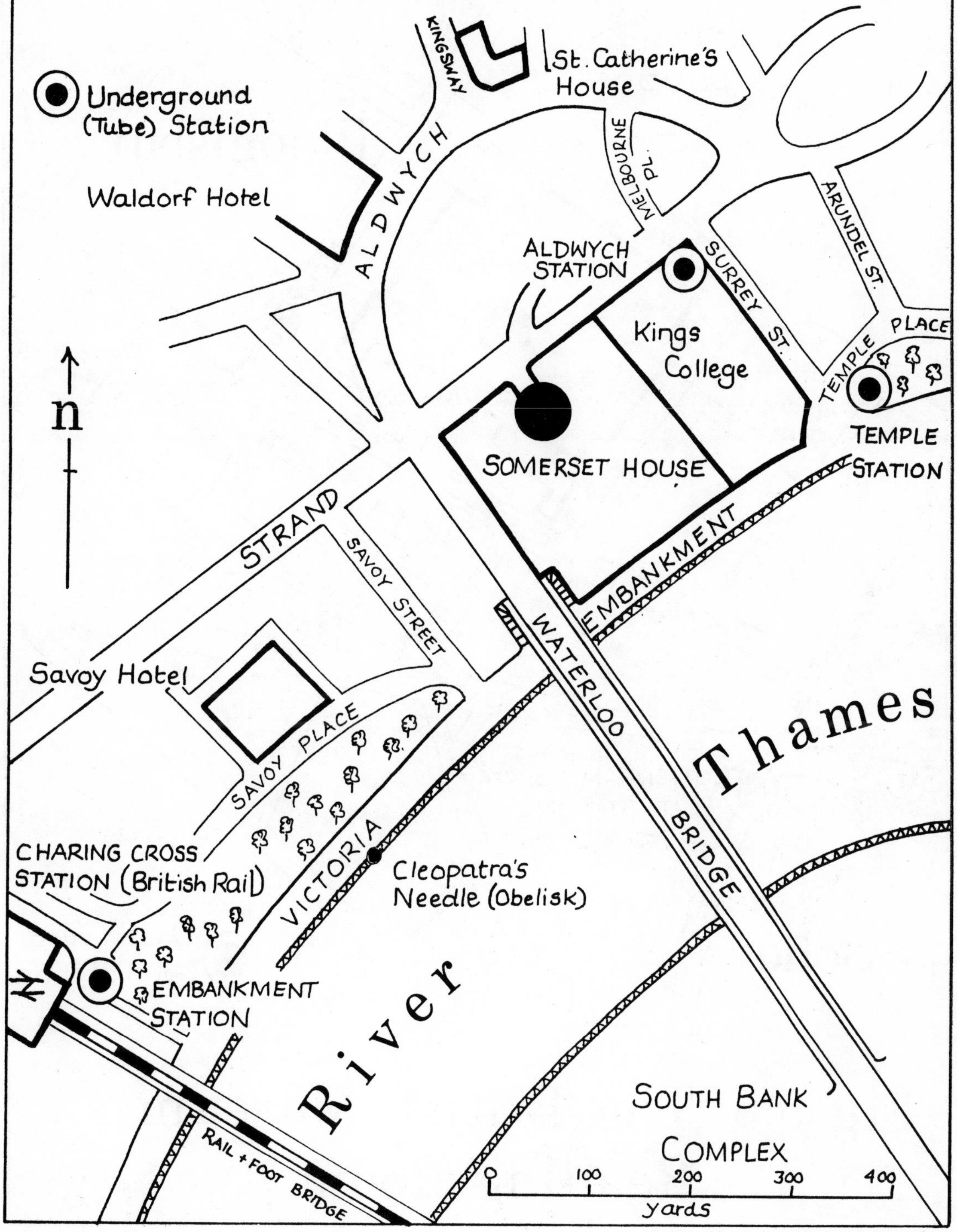

- ⦿ Underground (Tube) Station
- Waldorf Hotel

KINGSWAY

St. Catherine's House

ALDWYCH

MELBOURNE PL.

ALDWYCH STATION

SURREY ST.

ARUNDEL ST.

Kings College

TEMPLE PLACE

SOMERSET HOUSE

TEMPLE STATION

n

STRAND

EMBANKMENT

SAVOY STREET

WATERLOO BRIDGE

Savoy Hotel

SAVOY PLACE

Thames

CHARING CROSS STATION (British Rail)

VICTORIA

Cleopatra's Needle (Obelisk)

EMBANKMENT STATION

River

SOUTH BANK COMPLEX

RAIL + FOOT BRIDGE

100   200   300   400

yards

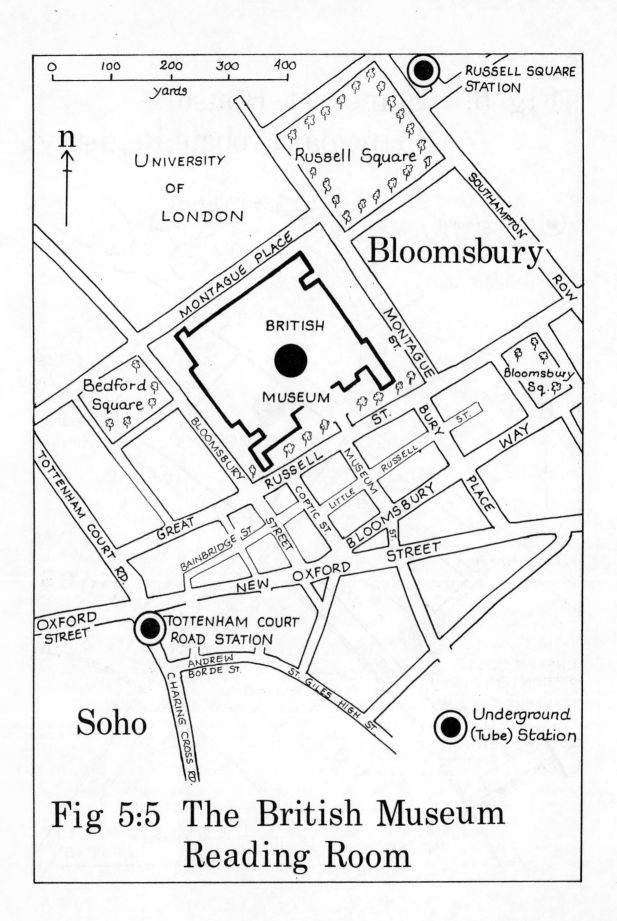

Fig 5:5 The British Museum
Reading Room

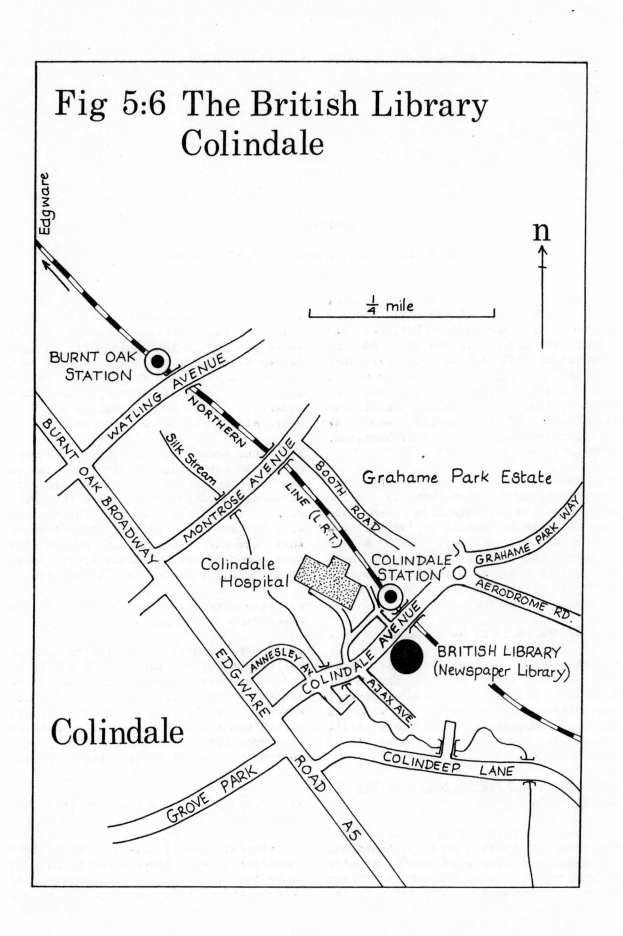

Fig 5:6 The British Library
Colindale

CHAPTER 6

RESEARCH IN AND AROUND THE PARISH CHURCH

The parish is probably the most ancient unit of ecclesiastical and civil administration in England. Parishes had almost certainly evolved by 1066 and many stand today in the boundaries they occupied in 1291. Thomas Cromwell, Henry VIII's Vicar-General, was the first to hint at a civil or administrative use of the parish when he instituted the registering of baptisms, marriages, and burials in 1538.

The Poor Law Act of 1601 created the 'civil' parish, which usually corresponded to the ecclesiastical one, and gave the parish council or 'vestry' new powers and obligations, which mainly concerned the care of the poor and indigent, thus creating a series of records about a class of society which would otherwise be undocumented.

Many of the parishes have deposited all their records at their county or diocesan record office, especially since the General Synod of the Church of England passed its 1978 measure requiring archival-quality depositories for such documents, but many still remain in the parishes. Fees or a donation are asked for searches.

Main Types Of Parish Record Of Use To Genealogists

a) Baptism, marriage and burial registers. Until the 19th century, baptisms, burials, and marriages were generally entered in one book, rather mixed and not easily searched. Very early regis-

ters may be in Latin. To determine the earliest date for which registers survive in your parish, consult A. M. Burke's, Key to the Ancient Parish Registers of England and Wales. Note that all marriages had to be performed in the Church of England, except Jews and Quakers, hence many Catholics and Nonconformists held two ceremonies.

a) Banns books: after 1753. 'Banns' refers to the notice of marriage called out in the parishes of the couple for three consecutive weeks before the wedding. These may give more information than the marriage register, but remember that the marriage may not necessarily have taken place! (Before 1753, banns were usually recorded in the register.)

c) Ratepayers' lists: a list of the ratepayers in the parish.

d) Vestry minutes. The vestry was the ruling body of the parsh. It appointed church wardens, constables, and overseers of the poor, and made regular reports. W. E. Tate, author of The Parish Chest states that "vestry minutes are among the most interesting of parish records." Do not forget their potential.

e) Overseers of the Poor records include:

-settlement certificates, almost like passports, that paupers had to have to move out of their town of origin. They were handed to the vestry of the new parish.

-account books. Up to 1834 these are very full, naming fathers of bastards, apprenticeships of pauper children, recording vagrant passes, and so on.

f) Apprenticeship records, mainly after 1757. Pauper children were apprenticed at cost to the parish and apprenticeship constituted legal 'settlement' in the parish. Apprenticeship indenturers give name of child and age, and domicile, name, parish, and trade of master, and years of indenture.

When a parish issued a certificate of settlement, it acknowledged its obligation to give relief to the recipient if they became a pauper. The settlement parish might not be the recipient's present address, but where he or she would be sent if impoverished.

g) Burial-in-woolen certificates (1666-1814). In 1666, Parliament enacted a law requiring burial in woolen and a certificate to show it, to promote Britain's flagging wool industry. Within eight days of burial, someone present at the funeral had to furnish the affidavit stating that the corpse's shroud had been woolen. Enforcement of the law did lapse some time before its repeal in 1814.

h) Censuses. Early censuses were carried out by parish constables and were sometimes copied into the parish register or vestry minutes.

Examples: poll-tax 1678-1679
            window-tax 1695-1851
            1641 Protestation Returns
            (listing males over 18)
            1801 Census

i) Tithe award maps depicting ownership within the parish.

j) Touching for the King's Evil. In 1626 an Act required a patient wishing to be touched by the King to bring a certificate from his priest and church-wardens stating he had not been 'touched' before. These certificates named the patient, and his parents or spouse. The custom was discontinued by George I in 1714.

k) Sketch-maps of pew arrangements were often made to settle arguments between rival claimants. Nearness to the altar indicated high social standing; though not of strict genealogical importance, such knowledge is nevertheless an interesting dimension to the family history.

Outside The Church

Unlike churches in the US, English churches are usually surrounded by the graveyard, another valuable source of information. However, only a small percentage of Englishmen have had head-stones erected, these being the wealthier elements of society, so do not expect 100% success in locating relevant tombstones. It is certainly worth a try, though. High boots or old shoes will be handy, for the ground may be muddy and nettles high.

Take along utensils for cleaning stones: a soft rag or old toothbrush will do in most cases, but keep cleaning to a minimum. Transcribe the inscriptions carefully - guesses are worse than useless. Try to describe the location of the stone; if time permits, make a sketch-map showing the exact location of each stone recorded.

You may wish to photograph the stone as a permanent record. A 35mm camera with adjustable focus and variable shutter speeds is best, using a slow black and white film. Color film has an estimated life of only 50 years and should not be used if you want your negatives to last. Use a flash if the light is poor.

Have the camera parallel to the stone; do not shoot from a standing position. Most importantly, practice before your trip (in varying lighting conditions), in your local cemetery. Eliminate the chance of error on 'the big day' when you find the headstone of your umpteenth great-grandfather!

Inside The Church

Take some time to explore the interior
of the parish church.   Most have memor-
ials such as rolls of honour from the
two World Wars.   You may be able to
purchase a parish history leaflet.
These are sources not to be overlooked.
The bonus is you'll be able to 'soak up'

the atmosphere once enjoyed each Sunday
by you ancestors! My greatest thrill in
genealogy was to visit, with my mother,
sister and children, Thursford Church in
Norfolk where we signed the visitors
book, "all above are descendants of
George Dunthorne and Esther Guyton,
married here 15 May 1791." That was
happiness!

CHAPTER 7

THE FAMILY HISTORY SOCIETY: TO JOIN OR NOT TO JOIN?

England is very fortunate to be served by over sixty local family history and genealogical societies. Hardly any part of the country is without a group to which you can turn for help, and some more populous counties can boast several societies. The oldest, the Society of Genealogists, is based in London with worldwide membership and has a long and scholarly history. For many years the Society was run on the lines of a gentleman's club, but with the burgeoning interest in genealogy since the 1960's, it has dusted off its image, opened itself up and has even moved from its venerable but cramped quarters in Kensington to a more spacious and utilitarian building in the East End of London. Membership applications must be supported by two sponsors, preferably members themselves, or by professional persons of your acquaintance. The cost is $43 for the first year, $28 per annum thereafter. If you do not wish to join the Society but would like to subrscibe to The Genealogists' Magazine (quarterly), you may do so at a cost of $20 per annum.

Locally-based societies are a great deal smaller than the Society of Genealogists; annual membership fees range from $10 to $15 for overseas members. The emphasis among these groups is family history, a broader-based subject than genealogy, but with genealogical research as its firm foundation.

What do you get for your money? Newsletters, interest and publication lists, and more.

All societies issue newsletters and journals. The Norfolk and Norwich Genealogical Society's quarterly, The Norfolk Ancestor is a sixteen page journal, with a professional appearance. Members are also sent a hard-cover annual work, such as transcripts of tax returns or parish records. The Birmingham and Midland Society for Genealogy and Heraldry publishes The Midland Ancestor quarterly, a forty page journal with regular columns such as 'Bookworm' and 'Census Strays', as well as articles from members. Most newsletters and journals carry a query column, in which members place ads (free or for a small fee) to help find missing ancestors.

Another useful tool published by many groups is a members' interest list. Members submit lists of surnames in which they are interested, and the reader can scan the list and write to members with whom he or she has a common interest. It would be very useful to establish communication with such people well before a planned visit to England, not only to enlist their aid but to establish a working relationship which could reach fruition during the visit.

According to the size of the society, it will have a smaller or larger publications list. These could include a local genealogical records guide, parish register transcripts, census indexes, monument inscriptions, maps, plus publications of national societies.

These publications are generally una-vailable except through the society and as they are in relatively small edi-tions, they become rare and worth their weight in gold.

For the person visiting England, there is access to genealogical society libra-ries. The size and quality of the col-lection will vary tremendously, depend-ing on the society. One library I vi-sited was in the chairman's cellar and had a very higgledy-piggledy aspect: there was a card catalogue, and even a section of the I.G.I., but the chairman was the only person able to locate ma-terial. Fortunately, he was obliging and helpful. Another society library I used was housed in the basement of an educational institution, was well organ-ized, and had on duty a volunteer to help members find what they needed.

Some larger societies have established postal lending libraries. This can be expensive but may be worth inquiring about. Generally, the lending library catalog is much shorter than the regular library's catalog.

The Birmingham and Midland Society goes a step further in helping new members by assigning each a correspondence secretary, to whom the new member can write with any questions or problems. This is an innovation which should be applauded and imitated.

The overseas member can benefit enormously through entitlement to the Federation of Family History Societies Accomodation Register. Only F.H.S. Members may buy a copy, which lists other members in most counties willing to offer bed and breakfast. Not only do you 'sleep cheap' (and probably in cozy comfort), but you also get to 'talk shop' and quite possibly benefit from your hosts' local knowledge. The advan-tages are obvious. Your copy may be obtained for $2.25 surface mail or $2.85 airmail from Mrs. C. Walcot, 1 Strode Manor Farm Cottages, Netherbury, Brid-port, Dorset DTG 5NG. Quote your socie-ty and membership number.

Remember that English genealogical and family history societies were not established as pedigree societies, such as the Daughters of the American Revolution, but they are manifestations of a keen interest in local history and a desire for self-knowledge.

NOTE: A complete list of Family History Societies with addresses is given in Appendix C.

CHAPTER 8

SOLVING SOME COMMON GENEALOGICAL PROBLEMS

This chapter will explore some of the more common and frustrating problems which you may encounter during your research trip. I will suggest some solutions and hope that these will lead you to create your own answers, or spot your mistakes.

Unable To Locate A Subject's Birth Certificate

-check that your source of information for place is correct. If in doubt, go to the census nearest to that date and check for a street address. Remember, too, that Registration Districts were changed in 1852.

-check diverse spellings of both Christian and surnames. Did the subject have two forenames originally? They may have been juxtaposed, so be careful.

-child may have been registered with a totally different Christian name. My great-grandmother was always know as Annie Elizabeth. I completely failed to locate her birth certificate, though I did find her baptismal record. Some time later a great-aunt told me she had been registered as Harriet for some unkown reason, and so had had great difficulty proving, for social security reasons, her age!

-child may have been register with a different surname:
    a) if illegitimate
    b) to hide illegitimacy

c) if later adopted

Illegitimacy led to a great deal of lying to the authorities. The father of author Barbara Pym stated on his marriage certificate that he was the son of Thomas Pym, farmer, deceased. He was actually Thomas' grandson: his birth certificate showed he was the son of Phoebe Pym, a servant. No father's name was given on the certificate.

-registration was not compulsary until 1875 and many births were simply never registered.

-human error - did you read the indexes correctly or did you tire and miss some entries?

-cross-check with the I.G.I. and parish records.

-if you still cannot locate the child's entry, settle for that of a brother or sister. The same basic information will be given.

Unable To Locate A Marriage Certificate

Marriage records can be difficult and tedious to locate at St. Catherine's House if you are searching a common name, or if your information is incomplete; e.g., missing the bride's first and maiden name. There are, however, other reasons for failure.

-are the names of the parties correct? Check various spellings and any ali-

47

ases; e.g., name by a previous marriage, or adoption.

-could they have married elsewhere? Check adjacent parishes and nearby large cities. My grandmother married in a Birmingham church though she lived in the rural parish of Clent.

-check other years. People have often falsified statements orally and in family bibles to hide a 'shot-gun wedding.'

-are you sure a wedding ever took place? Even if its intent was recorded in banns books or a liscense issued, this does not mean for certain that it happened.

-human error - did you read carefully enough?

-human error - was the marriage wrongly indexed? Try to imagine the possibilities.

-censuses - check where the first child was born. This could provide a valuable clue to the place and time of the marriage.

Unable To Locate A Death Certificate

-start at the latest possible date. This can be established from the censuses, or at least ninety years after the birth date. Work backwards, always bearing in mind the person's age.

-if the subject was widowed, she may have remarried and died under a different name. Check the marriage indexes.

-did the person possibly die abroad or in military service? St. Catherine's has separate registers for deaths at sea and abroad. The War Office has a list of deaths during World War I, and earlier Armed Services records are in the Public Record Office.

-check at the Principal Probate Registry for a will. This would help pinpoint a

date and place of death.

-human error - have you read the indexes carefully enough.

-human error - the information on death certificates can only be as good as the informant. This may not have been a close relative; errors in spellings and facts can ensue.

-alternative sources of information include burial registers, undertakers' records, obituaries and monumental inscriptions.

Mother's Maiden Name Not Known

Try to locate a marriage certificate or record:

a) check the I.G.I. in London; this is housed in Exhibition Road and the Society of Genealogists.
b) check the Pallot Index. This covers the years 1780-1837 and is especially strong for the London marriages (101 of 103 ancient parishes have been covered); forty English counties are also included. The Pallot Index is housed at the Institute of Genealogical and Heraldic Studies in Canterbury. (See Appendix D) There is a fee for each search.
c) check Boyd's marriage index, either at the L.D.S. library or the Society of Genealogists.

-did the subject or her husband or siblings leave a will? Check at the Principal Probate Registry. A will can give clues to her family's name and location.

-did the subject's children have any unusual middle names?

-check for the existence of a passport and re-check any family papers for clues you may have missed.

Failure To Find An Individual In The Census

The source of your address information,

a certificate, newspaper clipping, etc., will very likely be out of date by the next census. You can:

-search a city directory of a date near to the census date.

-search the electoral rolls available at the C.R.O.

-if a small town, search its census records and those of adjacent towns. Be diligent, it can be very time consuming.

-human errors - on your part or that of the census-enumerator?

-check I.G.I., Boyd's, or the Pallot Index.

-could the person have lived in another household; for example, as a servant or visitor?

-a good knowledge of local and socio-economic history might give clues as to the direction of migration. Wars, for example, have often had a profound effect on migration patterns.

When you come across an apparently insurmountable problem, do not feel defeated. Spread the facts out, sort them, analyze, and make a plan to get around the problem. Your answer may be buried deep in an index or a roll of microfilm, but if you do not look, you will never find it.

You Wish To Search One Of The Censuses 1891-1901

It is possible to obtain details of specific individuals named on censuses not yet released for general use. You must write to the Registrar General at St. Catherine's House, Kingsway, London W.I., enclosing ₤15. You must state your purpose and that the subject is either dead or assents to the search, and you must supply the exact address of the subject. (This can be obtained from a registrar's certificate, burial or baptismal record, or electoral rolls at the C.R.O.)

CHAPTER 9

INTERPRETING THE PAST

Interpretation Of Ancient Documents

Major obstacles in the reading of pre-nineteenth century records certainly exists for the genealogist unless he or she happens to have studied Latin and paleography. It is essential to study and be prepared before visiting archives or record offices; archivists are not there to be your personal record interpreter, that is your job! I shall try to make the task lighter by taking each obstacle, step-by-step, and give exercises to help with each. Go over the exercises consientiously and repeat them at intervals.

Spelling

We tend to take uniformity in spelling for granted, so you may be surprised to find out it is actually a very recent innovation. Before the nineteenth century and the movement towards public education, literate people were few and far between, and they tended to make up their own spelling as they wrote. It is not uncommon to find the same word spelled differently within the same sentence!

From my personal experience, I feel the best approach here is to use you imagination together with contextual clues. 'Hear' the word as it would have been spoken, rather than trying to use the phonics rules you were taught in school, and ignore odd capital letters.

All answers are at the end of the chapter.

Exercise 1A

Write the following phrases in modern English.

a) Itm one lynnen cloth
b) Itm one diapur Napkyn
c) Itm one Bason
d) Itm one Servyse boke
e) Itm one Surples, for the Person

Exercise 1B

Write the following phrases in modern English,

a) Elizabeth Smyth wyff of Jno was burried the xijth of Marche
b) Anne borne of a wayfaringe woman was xd the xxth of Marche
c) Jan Wagit wyff of Tho: was buryed the xxvith daye of Novembre.
d) Wyllm Dunkhorne and Merry hunt war Maried the xxth of April.

Archaic Terms

Archaic words are words no longer in use. Generally, the meaning of such words can be conjectured from the context of the piece. For example: 'leasowe' which I discovered in the inventory of a seventeenth-century ancestor, I inferred meant 'meadow' as the rest of the section was concerned with agricultural assets. The Oxford English Dictionary later confirmed my conjecture.

Below is a list of some other common archaic words. For words not listed here, refer to the Oxford English Dictionary which should be available at your library.

ambery/aumbry - small cupboard
band - 'bond', agreement
bandcloth - linen collar
beares, beres - pillowcases
bease - cattle
bed hillings - bedclothers
ben - hardware
chaffingdish - cooking dish
cordwood - firewood
deyhouse - dairy
form - bench
fustian - type of cloth
gawne - gallon pail
hogshead - 54 gallons
hutch - small chest for clothes
keep - a safe
lather - ladder
leasowe - meadow
press - cupboard - wardrobe
pullen - poultry
quern - hand-mill
spence - larder
tramells - instrument for lowering & raising a kettle over a fire
trestells - a beam
trivett - a three legged cooking stand
trussing bed - trendle bed
twilleys - woolen material
virginals - small harpsichord
whitch - coffer

Abbreviations And Contractions

Because wills, registers, and legal documents were couched in jargon, it became the common practice to use abbreviations and contractions for syllables and whole words. These can be divided into several types.

1) Letters ommitted completely - this was indicated by a mark above the word, an apostrophe, or mark below the word.

Examples: com̃on - common
Dm̃i - Domini
Willm̃ - William
M̃garet - Margaret

Letters omitted (continued)

p̲fect - perfect
p̲rede - precede
p̲pose - propose
p'jury - perjury

2) Superior letters - the word is shortened by ommision of a vowel and placing some of letters above the line.

Examples: wth - with
w^{ch} - which
we^{r} - were
y^{t} - that
y^{e} - the

Note: 'y' in the last two examples is a remnant of the Anglo-Saxon letter for 'th'.

3) Final letters ommitted - this is usually represented by a period, semi-colon, or colon.

Examples: fro: - from
wid. - widow
ite; - item

4) Abbreviated names. Christian names were frequently abbreviated to save time, generally according to the rules above.

Example: J^{no} - John
Rich^{r}d - Richard
Rob̲t - Robert
Tho: - Thomas
W^{m} - William
Thom̃s - Thomas
x̄pofer - Christopher
Saml - Samuel
Edwd - Edward

Handwriting

Handwriting has changed almost beyond recognition since the Tudor Age and can be the genealogist's greates challenge. It is not, however, an unsuperable one. Many English-speaking children learn to read and write fluently in Russian, Hebrew, and Greek, none of which uses the Roman alphabet. In paleography, we are using the Roman alphabet - the letter formations are simply different or

GENERAL ALPHABET

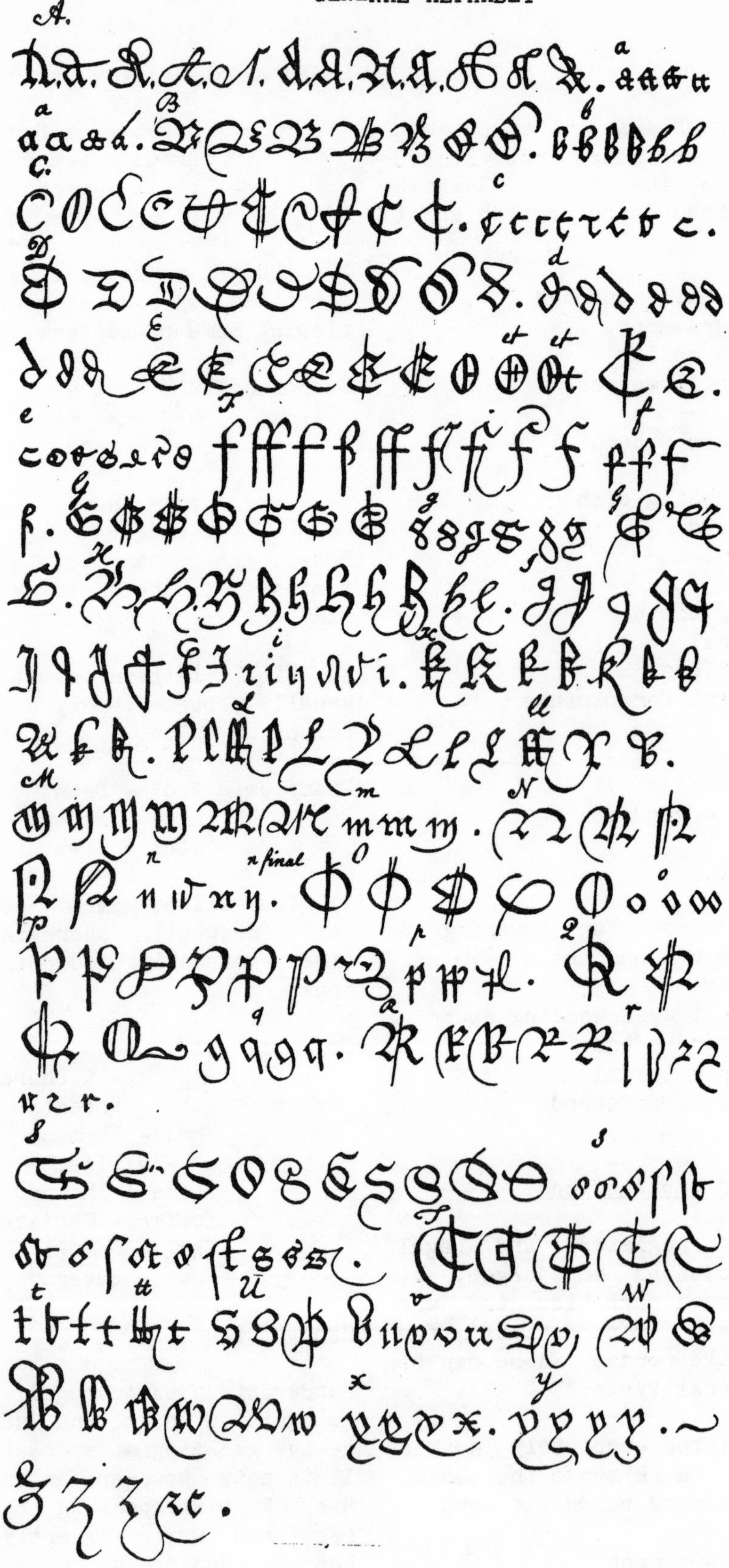

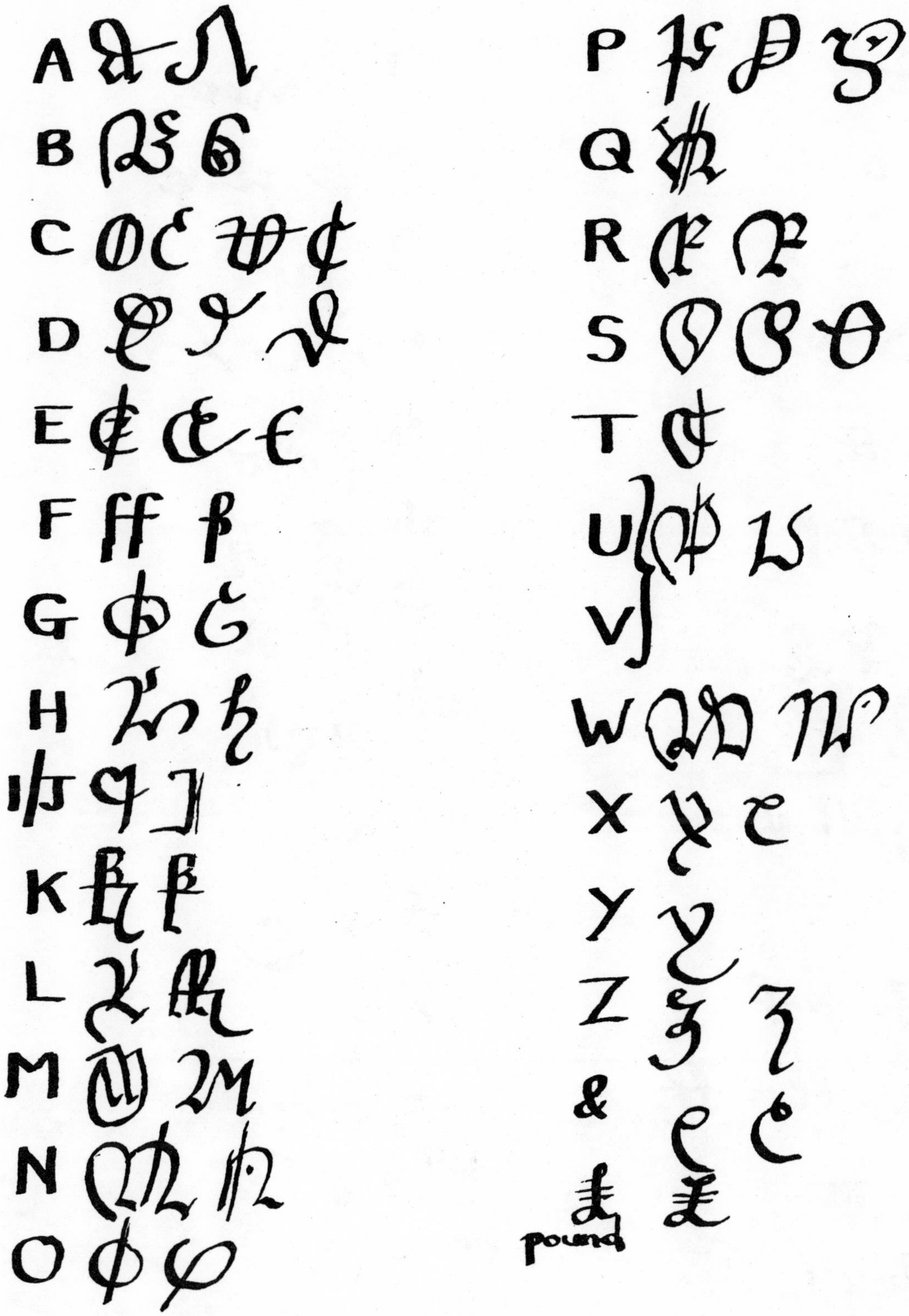

Fig. 9A

LOWER-CASE LETTERS

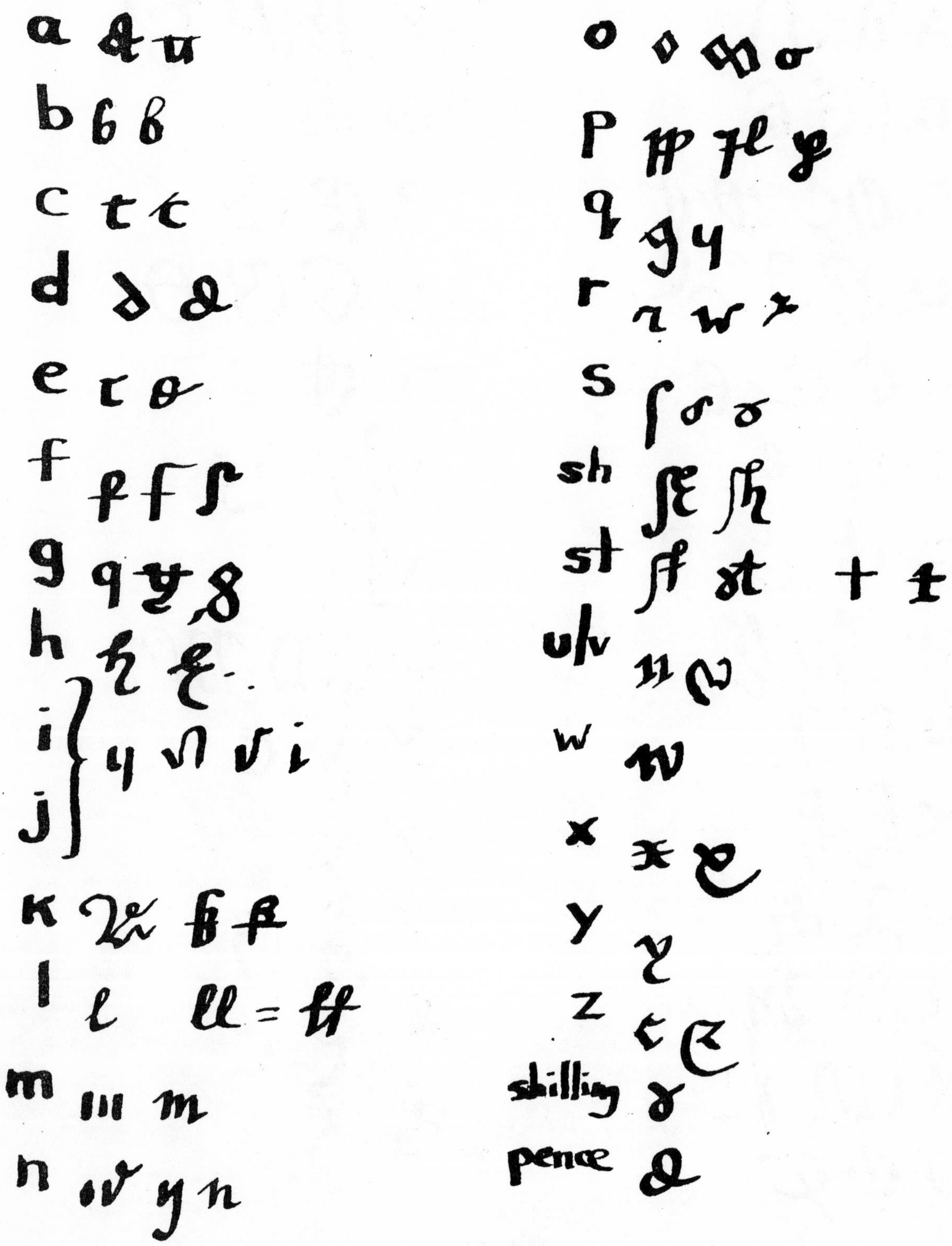

Fig. 9A

1	i or j	15	xv
2	ij	20	xx
3	iij	21	xxj
4	jv or iv	25	xxv
5	v	30	xxx
6	vj	50	L
7	vij	51	Lj
8	viij	90	xc
9	jx or ix	100	c
10	x/e	101	cj
11	xj	200	cc
12	xij	1000	m

Fig. 9A

more diverse than we, in the age of print, are used to.

1) The Secretary Alphabet

In Fig. 9A are various common forms of each letter. Use a narrow calligraphic nib to copy each letter at least fifty times. When you are sure you know the letter forms, try writing the alphabet without reference to the model. Go back to Exercise 1 and write them out using your new skills.

2) Recognizing Whole Words

After a good deal of alphabet practice, you should be ready to begin 'decoding' whole words. This is actually more difficult than to read whole sentences, because a sentence will usually furnish you with contextual clues. In Fig. 9B are individual words from 17th century documents you will be reading later on. You may refer back to your practice alphabets the first time only. Later, try the section again without reference help. When you can 'read' the examples naturally, you will be ready to proceed to the next section.

3) Practice In Reading Documents

Plates 1 and 2 are examples of typical documents you will be reading. Skim them first, to get the broad sense of the document, then go back and make a word-for-word transcription. Keep to the lines used in the original and do not alter spelling or expand contractions. Full transcriptions are given at the end of the chapter.

A Note On Dates

Prior to 1753, New Year's Day was held to be March 25th. Therefore, March 24th, 1642 would have been, according to our present calendar March 24th, 1643 (pushing New Year's Day back to January 1st). Exercise caution, therefore, when dating a document which precedes the 19th century. If necessary, write the modern date in parentheses.

Exercise 2

Change to the modern dating system, if necessary:

   I) April 12, 1672
  II) February 21st, 1578
 III) October 9th, 1706
  IV) January 3rd, 1627
   V) November 11th, 1780

Problem: how could a baby have been baptized on November 21st, 1550 and been buried March 2nd, 1550?

Reading And Interpreting Latin

Latin was the legal and ecclesiastical language of Europe throughout the Middle Ages and remained dominant until the eighteenth century. Even if you do not intend to engage in medieval research, you may well come across parish registers and wills in Latin.

Many English words are derived from Latin and their meaning can be inferred. For example, the Latin 'obiit' and English 'obituary' have a common root meaning 'death'. Many words have also changed meaning over the cenuries, though, so exercise caution when translating. A comprehensive Latin word list is given in Appendix F.

Notes On Latin Grammar

1) Nouns and adjectives
   Nouns can be either:
   masculine: ending in - us (e.g. dominus)
   feminine: ending in - a (e.g. puella)
   neuter: ending in - um (e.g. bellum)

The adjective then 'agrees' with the noun and has the same ending.

Example: puella bona - a good girl
        dominus bonus - a good lord

Many words can be masuline or feminine - judge by the ending.

'Sobrinus' is a male cousin, 'sobrina' is a female cousin. In the word list this is indicated as 'sobrina/us'.

Some nouns end in other ways, such as -er, -is, or -es. All nouns 'decline', that is, change their ending according to their position in the sentence.

Examples: Puella videt agricolam.
The girl sees a farmer.

BUT   Agricola videt puellam.
The farmer sees the girl.

In Fig. 9C is a table of the most common endings.

2) Verbs

Latin verbs do not need pronouns such as 'I' or 'we': these pronouns are indicated by the ending of the verb. In the word list, you will find the 'I' form of the verb, as it is easier to work out the other forms from this. Occasionally pronouns were used for emphasis: ego (I), te (you), nos (we).

Present tense of portare (to carry):
   I: porto
 you: portas
  he: portat
  we: portamus
 you: portatis
they: portant

Future: take the infinitive (portare) and drop the 're'. This is your future root.

portabo - I will carry
portabis - you will carry
portabit - he will carry
portabimus - we will carry
portabitis - you will carry
portabunt - they will carry

Past: take the root (porta) and add the endings.

portavi - I carried
portavisti - you carried
portavit - he carried
portavimus - we carried
portavistis - you carried
portaverunt - they carried

3) Medieval Spelling

Written Latin, like written English, was not uniform; words were often spelled phonetically. If you cannot translate a word, try to work out alternative spellings.

Main substitutions are:
j for i
i for e
v for u
s for c

4) Medieval Dating

The Church's calendar of feasts and saints' days were used in preference to the Roman calendar. So, rather than write February 2nd, a scribe would write 'Candlemas' or one of its Latin names. Appendix F lists most major feast days. If you are flummoxed by an unknown saint, refer to the Catholic Encyclopedia.

5) Numerals

Words for numbers are included in Appendix F. Numbers were written thus:

j	1	vij	7	xx	20	xc	90
ij	2	viij	8	xxx	30	c	100
iij	3	ix	9	xl	40	cm	900
iv	4	x	10	l	50	m	1000
v	5	xj	11	lx	60		
vi	6	xij	12	xc	90		

Fig. 9C   TABLE OF THE MOST COMMON NOUN ENDINGS

	Masculine noun		Feminine noun		Neuter noun	
	Singular	Plural	Singular	Plural	Singular	Plural
Subject	dominus	domini	puella	puellae	castrum	castra
Object	dominum	dominos	puellam	puellas	castrum	castra
'of the'	domini	dominorum	puellae	puellarum	castri	castrorum
'to the'	domino	dominis	puellae	puellis	castro	castris

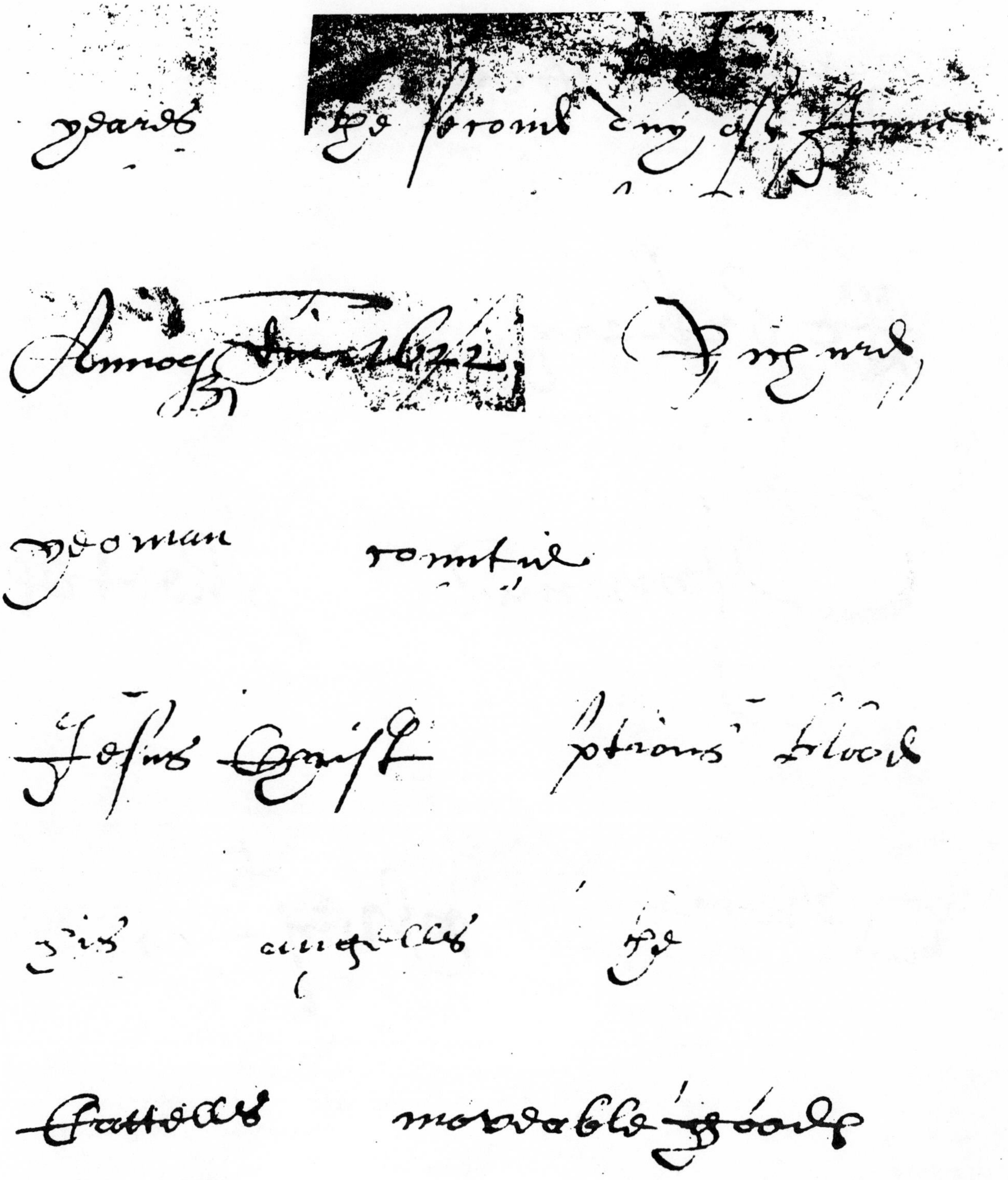

Fig. 9B

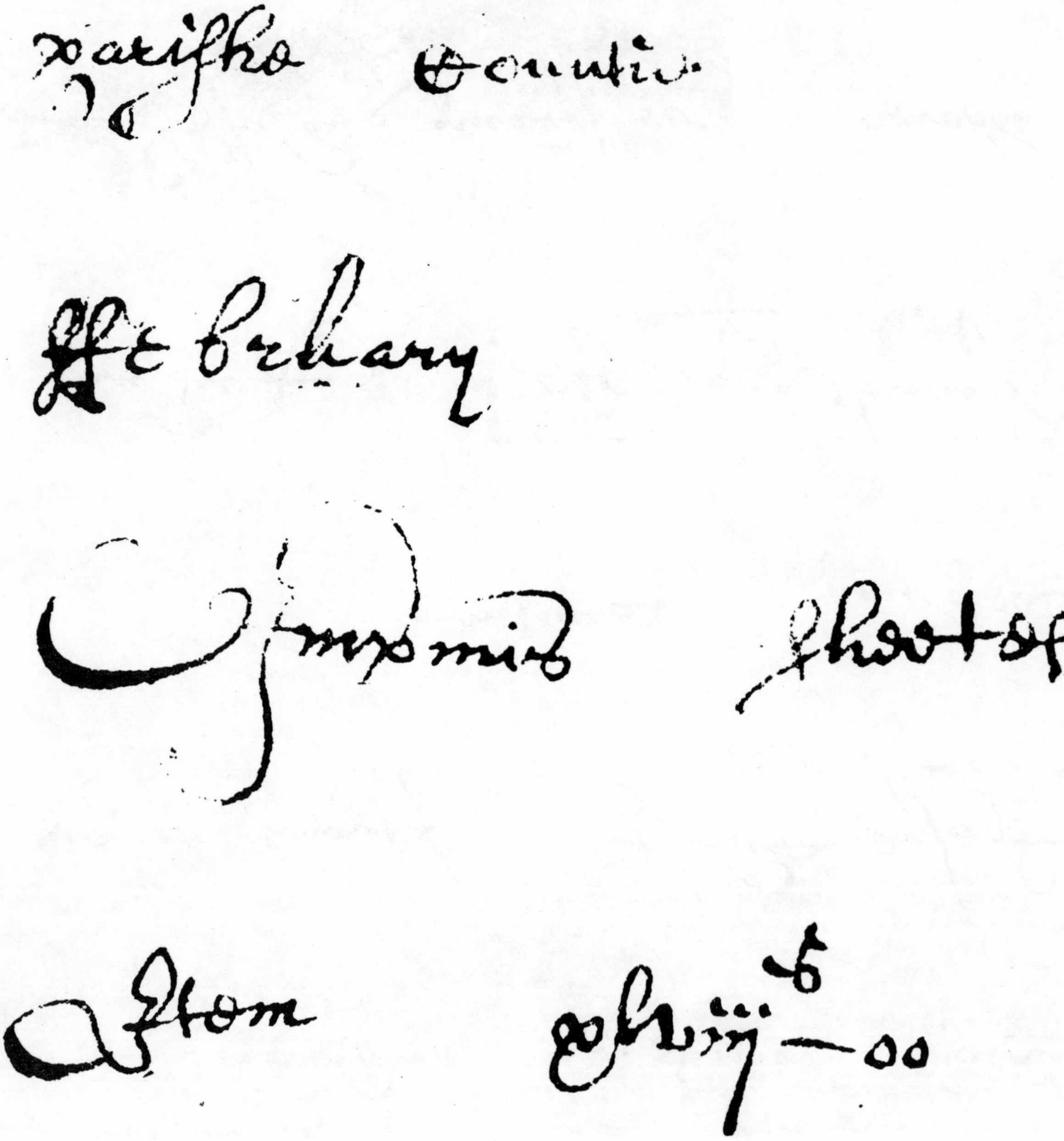

Fig. 9B

A true Inventary of y[e] goodes of Roger Warkman late of woodrote in the parishe of Bromsgrove in the County of Worcester, praysed, apprayҫed by the partie vnder named the sixth day of this present ffebruary Anno Domi 1642 : Annoq[ue] R[egis] Car[oli] xviij[th] in manner following viz

Imprimis his wearinge apparell and money in his purҫe the ҫume of _____ x[li] - 00

Item in the [par]ler nine sheetes one table clothe halfe a dozen of table napkinҫ a coverlet rugge and dalet three ҫmall diҫhes of powter at the ҫume of _____ xx[s] - 00

Item in the greate barne in corne hay and ҫtrawe att the ҫume of _____ xx[li] - 00

Item in the Littell barne hay att the ҫume of xviij[s] - 00

Item corne growing on acre of land called the Lyttell wheate leaҫowe att the ҫume of xx[li] - 00

Item things that may be forgotten and not apraysd ---00[s]-- vj[d]

Somma totius --- xij[li] --- viij[s] vj[d]

The aprayҫor
Robert Wylle
Thomas Haightinge
John Chellingworthe

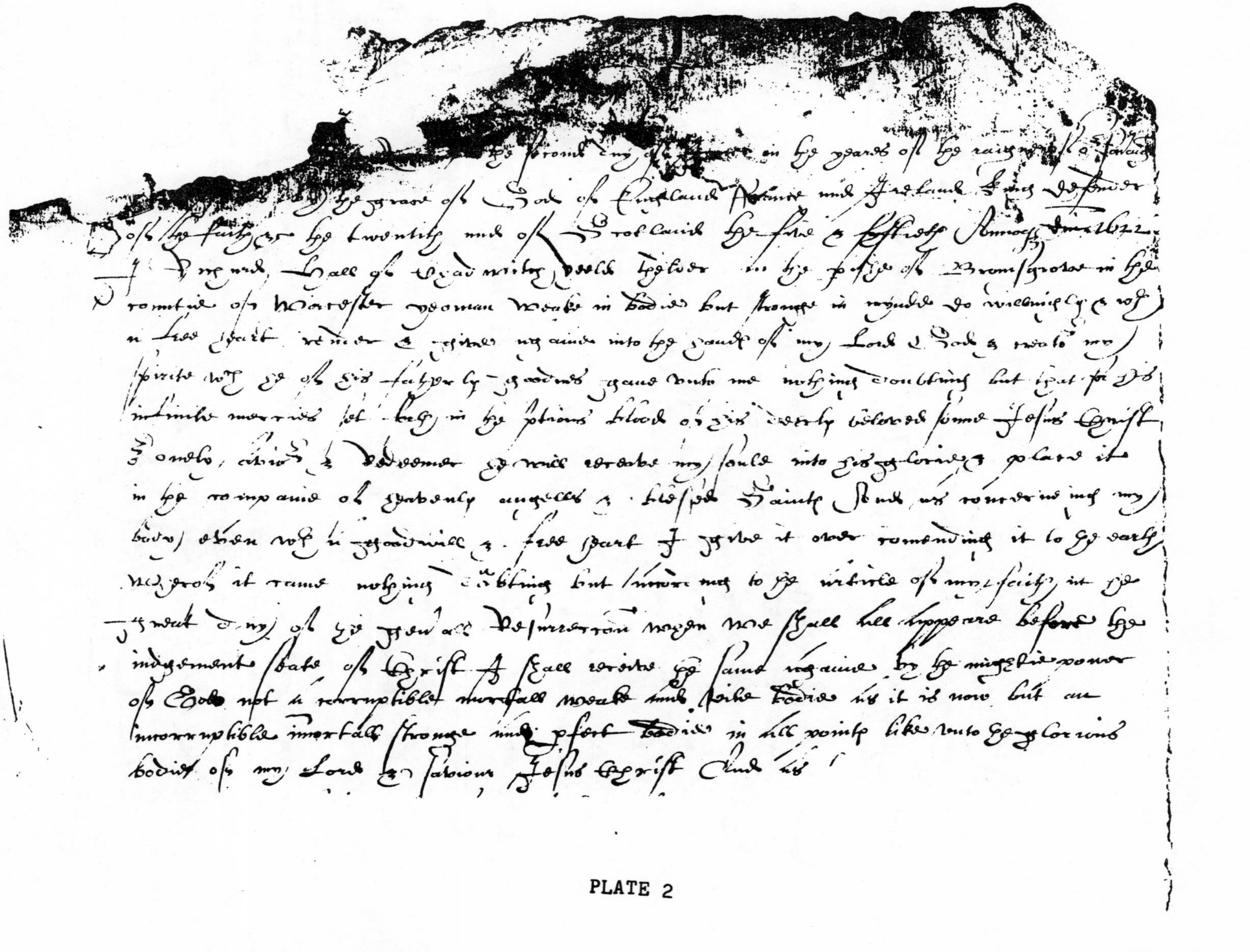

PLATE 2

Answers To Exercises In This Chapter

Exercise:

1A a) Item one linen cloth
   b) Item one diaper napkin
   c) Item one basin
   d) Item one service book
   e) Item one surplice, for the parson

Exercise:

1B a) Elizabeth Smith wife of John was buried the 12 of March.
   b) Anne born of a wayfaring woman was christened the 20th of March
   c) Jane Waggett wife of Thomas was buried the 26 day of November
   d) William Dunthorne and Mary Hunt were married the 20 of April

Fig 9B

    I) yeare
   II) second day of June
  III) Anno Domini 1622
   IV) Richard
    V) yeoman
   VI) countie
  VII) Jesus Christ
 VIII) precious blood
   IX) his
    X) angelles
   XI) the
  XII) chattelles
 XIII) movable goods
  XIV) parishe
   XV) countie
  XVI) February
 XVII) Imprimis
XVIII) nine sheets
   XX) item
  XXI) XXVIIIs - 00

Plate 1

A true inventory of ye goodes of Roger Wakeman late of Woodcote in the parishe of Bromsgrove in the countie of Worcestershire deceased, aprasysed by the prices under named the sixth day of this ffebruary Ann^o Domi 1642: xviii^{th} in manner ffollowinge

	S	D
Imprimis his warminge apparell and money in his purse the sume of	xx	oo

Itm in the $\underline{p}ler^1$
nine sheetes one table cloth
halfe duzen of table napkines
a pewter cuppe and three
small pieces of pewter at the

sume of	xx	oo
Item in the greate barne in corn and hay and strawe att the sume of	xx	oo
Item in the littell barne haye att the sume of	xviii	oo
Item corne growinge in a/$\underline{p}cell^2$ of land called the lyttell wheate leasowe at the sume of	xx	oo
Item things that maybe for gotten and not ap^raysed	oo	vj^d

suma vi^h $viij^s$ vj^d

The ap^raysers
  Robert Wylde
  Thomas ffaighting
  John Chellingworth

1. parlour
2. a parcel

Plate 2

(In the name of) God Amen the second day of June in the yeare of the raigne of 0^r sovreign Lord James by the grace of God of England, France, and Ireland King defender of the faith...the twentieth and of Scotland the five and fortieth Anno Dmi 1622. I Richard Hall of Chadwich yeeld (thelder?) in the $prshe^1$ of Bromsgrove in the countie of Worcester yeoman weake in bodie but stronge in mynde do willingly and wth a full heart $reme{r}$ and give againe into the hands of my Lord God and $creat^r$ my spirite wch he of his fatherly goodness gave unto me nothing doubting but that for his infinite mercies...in the $pcious^2$ blood of his dearly beloved sonne Jesus Christ 0^r only savior and redeemer he will receave my soule into his glorie and place it in the companie of heavenly angelles and blessed Sainte Ann and commending it to the earth whereof it came nothing doubting but trusting to the...of my faith and the great day of the generall Resurrection when we shall all appeare before the iudgement seate of Christ and shall receave the same againe by the mightie power of God not a corruptible mortall weake and sicke bodie as it is now but an incorruptible immortall stronge and pfect bodie in all points like unto the glorious bodie of my Lord and Saviour Jesus Christ.

1 parish
2 precious

Exercise 2

    I) April 12th 1672
   II) February 21st, 1579
  III) October 9th, 1706
  IV) January 3rd, 1628
   V) November 11th, 1780

The baby was baptized in November 1550. In January, we begin dating 1551 but people then figured 1551 to bein on March 25th. Therefore March 2nd would have been written as 1550.

EPILOGUE

Tracing your genealogy and family history is a fascinating past-time and I hope that the reader will find the guidance in this book both informative encouraging. The fabric of history has been woven by millions of individuals and their lives deserve to be recorded. Many left evidence of their movements and actions in censuses, parish registers, vestry minutes, and poll, even if they themselves were illiterate. It is our task to unearth this evidence and place it in logical sequence.

It is my hope that the section on archaic script and language will not disconcert but will leave you with a feeling of accomplishment at mastering virtually a new language. If you wish to learn more about paleography, please refer to the bibliography.

The hints for traveling genealogists have been a result of my own experiences and I sincerely hope that they aid the you in planning and implementing a successful research trip. Enjoy your visit to the old country - may it be fruitful and happy!

BIBLIOGRAPHY

Burke, A.M. *Key To The Ancient Parish Registers*. London, 1908.

Cox, Jane and Padfield, Timothy. *Tracing Your Ancestors In The Public Record Office*. London: Her Majesty's Stationery Office, 1981.

Emmison, F.G. *Archives And Local History*. London: Methuen, 1966.

Emmison, F.G. *How To Read Local Archives 1550-1700*. London: Historical Association, 1967.

Gardner, D.E. et al. *Genealogical Research In England And Wales*. Salt Lake City, UT: Bookcraft, 1956-1959.

Grieve, Hilda. *Examples Of English Handwriting 1150-1750*. Essex Record Office, 1966.

West, John. *Village Records*. London: Phillimore, 1962, 1982.

Tate, W.E. *The Parish Chest*. Cambridge University Press, 1960.

APPENDIX A

COUNTY AND LOCAL RECORD OFFICES

* denotes Saturday hours; inquire for particulars

Bedfordshire
Bedfordshire County Record Office, County Hall, Bedford MK42 9AP; tel: Bedford 63222 ext. 277

Berkshire
Berkshire Record Office, Shire Hall, Reading, Berkshire RG1 3EE; tel: Reading 55981

Bristol
see Gloucestershire

Birmingham
see West Midlands

Buckinghamshire
Buckinghamshire Record Office, County Hall, Aylesbury, Buckingham-shire HP20 1VA; tel: Aylesbury 5000

Cambridgeshire
Cambridge County Record Office, Shire Hall, Cambridge CB1 0AP; tel: Cambridge 58811 ext 281

Cambridge University Archives, West Road, Cambridge CB3 9DR

Wisbech and Fenland Museum, Museum Square, Wisbech, Cambridgeshire; tel: 0945-583817

Cheshire
Cheshire Record Office*, The Castle, Chester CH1 2DN; tel: 061 480 2966

Cornwall
Cornwall County Record Office*, County Hall, Truro, Cornwall TR1 3AY; tel: Truro 74282

Cumberland
Cumbria County Record Office, The Castle, Carlisle CA3 8UR; tel: Carlisle 23456 ext 316

Derbyshire
Derbyshire Record Office*, County Offices, Matlock, Derbyshire DE4 3AG; tel: Matlock 3411

Devon
Devon County Record Office, Castle Stret, Exeter EX4 3BQ; tel: Exeter 79146

Devon Record Office (for West Devon), 14, Tavi-stock Place, Plymouth, Devon PL4 8AN; tel: Ply-mouth 28293

Dorset
Dorset County Record Office, County Hall, Dorchester, Dorset DT1 1XJ; tel: Dorchester 3131

Durham
Durham County Record Office, County Hall, Durham DH1 5UL; tel: Durham 64411

Darlington Public Library, Crown Street, Darlington DL1 1ND; tel: Darlington 69858

Essex
Essex Record Office, County Hall, Chelmsford, Essex CM1 1LX; tel: Chelmsford 67222

Gloucestershire
Gloucestershire County Record Office, Worcester Street, Gloucester GL1 3DW; tel: Gloucester 21444 ext 229

Bristol City Record Office*, The Council House, College Green, Bristol BS1 5TR; tel: Bristol 26031 ext 442

Hampshire
Hampshire Record Office, 20 Southgate Street, Winchester, Hampshire SO23 9EF; tel: Winchester 63153

Portsmouth City Record Office, The Guildhall, Portsmouth, Hampshire PO1 2AL; tel: Portsmouth 21771

Southampton Civic Record Office, Civic Centre, Southampton SO9 4XL; tel: Southampton 23855

Hereford
Hereford Record Office, The Old Barracks, Harold Street, Hereford HR1 2QX; tel: Hereford 65441

Hertfordshire
Hertfordshire Record Office, County Hall, Room 200 Library Block, Hartford SG13 8DE; tel: Hertford 54242

Humberside
see Lincolnshire and Yorkshire

Huntingdonshire
Huntingdonshire County Record Office, Grammar School Walk, Huntingdon PE18 6LF; tel: Huntingdon 52181

Kent
Kent Archives Office, County Hall, Maidstone, Kent ME11 1XH; tel: Maidstone 67411 ext 3312

Cathedral Archives and Library, The Precincts, Canterbury, Kent CT1 2EG; tel: Canterbury 63510

Diocesan Registry, The Precincts, Rochester, Kent; tel: Medway 4323

Institute of Heraldic and Genealogical Studies, Northgate, Canterbury, Kent; tel: Canterbury 68664

Lancashire
Lancashire County Record Office, Bow Lane, Preston, Lancashire PR1 8ND; tel: Preston 51905

Archives Department, Manchester Public Libraries, Central Library, St. Peter's Square, Manchester M2 5PD; tel: Manchester 236 7401

Liverpool Record Office*, Brown Picton and Homly Libraries, William Brown Street, Liverpool L3 8EW; tel: Liverpool 207 2147

Leicestershire
Leicestershire Record Office, 57, New Walk, Leicester LE1 7JB; tel: Leicester 539111

Lincolnshire
Lincolnshire Record Office, The Castle, Lincoln LN1 3AB; tel: Lincoln 25158

South Humberside Area Record Office*, Central Library, Town Hall Square, Grimsby, S. Humberside DN31 1HG; tel: Grimsby 59161 ext. 253

London and Middlesex
Greater London Record Office, The County Hall, London SE1 7PB; tel: 01 633 8186 or 7808

Middlesex County Records: Greater London Record Office, 1, Queen Anne's Gate Buildings, Dartmouth Street, London SW1Y 9BS

Corporation of London Records:
Guildhall, London EC2P 2EJ; tel: 01 606 3030

Lambeth Palace Library, London SE1 7JU

Norfolk
Norfolk Record Office*, Central Library, Norwich NR2 1NJ; tel: Norwich 22211 ext 599

see also Cambridgeshire Wisbech and Fenland Museum

Northamptonshire
Northamptonshire Record Office and Southwell Diocesan Record Office*, County House, High Pavement, Nottingham NG1 1HR; tel: Nottingham 54524

Oxfordshire
Oxfordshire County Record Office, County Hall, New Road, Oxford OX1 1ND; tel: Oxford 49861

Bodleian Library, Oxford OX1 3BG; tel: Oxford 44675

Oxford Central Library, Westgate, Oxford; tel: Oxford 722422

Rutland
see Leicestershire

Shropshire
Shropshire County Record Office, The Shirehall, Abbey Foregate, Shrewsbury SY2 6ND; tel: Shrewsbury 222406

Somerset
Somerset County Record Office*, Obridge Road, Taunton, Somerset TA2 7PU; tel: Taunton 87600

Bath City Record Office, The Guildhall, Bath BA4 5AW; tel: Bath 28411 ext 201

Staffordshire
Staffordshire County Record Office, County Buildings, Eastgate Street, Stafford ST16 2LZ; tel: Stafford 3121 ext 7923

Lichfield Joint Record Office, Lichfield Library, Bird Street, Lichfield WS13 6PN; tel: Lichfield 56787

Suffolk
East - Suffolk County Record Office*, County Hall, Ipswich IP4 2JS; tel: Ipswich 55801

West - Suffolk County Record Office*, Schoolhall Street, Bury St. Edmunds IP33 1RX; tel: Bury St. Edmunds 63141

Surrey
Surrey County Record Office, County Hall, Kingston-upon-Thames, Surrey KT1 2DN; tel: 01 546 1050 ext 3561

Sussex
East Sussex County Records Office, Pelham House, St. Andrew's Lane, Lewes, East Sussex BN7 1UN; tel: Lewes 5400

West Sussex County Record Office and Chichester Diocesan Record Office, County Hall, Chichester, West Sussex PO19 1RN; tel: Chichester 85100 ext 351

Warwickshire
Warwickshire County Record Office*, Priory Park, Cape Road, Warwick CV34 4JS; tel: Warwick 493431 ext 2508

Coventry City Record Office, 9, Hay Lane, Coventry CV1 5RF

West Midlands
Birmingham Reference Library, Central Library, Paradise Circus, Queensway, Birmingham; tel: 021 235 3591

Westmoreland
Westmoreland County Record Office, Council Offices, Kendal, Cumbria; tel: Kendal 21000

Isle of Wight
Isle of Wight County and Diocesan Record Office, 26, Hillside, Newport, Isle of Wight PO30 3EB; tel: Newport 4031 ext 32

Wiltshire
Wiltshire County Record Office, County Hall, Trowbridge, Wiltshire; tel: Trowbridge 3641 ext 3502

Diocesan Record Office, The Wren Hall, The Close, Salisbury, Wiltshire; tel: Salisbury 22519

Worcestershire
Worcestershire County Record Office, Shire Hall, Worcester; tel: Worcester 23400 ext 118

Yorkshire
North Yorkshire County Record Office, County Hall, Northallerton, North Yorkshire DL7 8SG; tel: Northallerton 3123 ext 455

West Yorkshire County Record Office, County Hall, Wakefield WF1 2QW; tel: Wakefield 67111 ext 2352

South Yorkshire County Record Office, Ellin Street, Sheffield S1 4PL; tel: Sheffield 29191 ext 33

Borthwick Institute of Historical Research, Peasholme Green, York YO1 2PV

Humberside County Record Office, County Hall, Beverly, N. Humberside; tel: Beverly 887131

Kingston-upon-Hull Record Office, Guildhall, Kingston-upon-Hull, N Humberside HU1 2AA; tel: Kingston-Upon-Hull 223111 ext 407

APPENDIX B

DENOMINATIONAL REPOSITORIES

Nonconformists in general:

Dr. William's Library, 14, Gordon Square, London WC1H OAG; tel: 01 387 1310

Specific nonconformist denominations:

United Reformed Church History Society, 86, Tavistock Place, London WC1; tel: 01 837 7661

Congregational Library, Memorial Hall, Farringdon Street, London EC4; tel: 01 236 2223

Baptist Union Library, 4, Southampton Row, London WC1; tel: 01 405 9803

Society of Friends Library, Friends House, Euston Road, London NW1; tel: 01 387 3601

Methodist Archives, Division of Property, Central Buildings, Oldham Street, Manchester M1 1JQ

Roman Catholicism

Catholic Record Society, c/o Miss R. Rendal, Flat 5, Lennox Gardens, London SW1X OBQ

Jewish Records

Jewish Museum, Woburn House, Upper Woburn Place, London WC1; tel 01 387 3081/2

APPENDIX C

MEMBERS OF THE FEDERATION OF FAMILY HISTORY SOCIETIES
IN GREAT BRITAIN AND THE UNITED STATES

Society of Genealogists
Mr. A. J. Camp, 14, Charterhouse Buildings, Goswell Road, London EC1M 7BA

Institute of Heraldic and Genealogical Studies
Miss S. Fincher, Northgate, Canterbury, Kent

Avon
see Bristol and Avon

Bedfordshire FHS
Mr. C. West, 17, Lombard St, Lidlington, Bedford MK43 0RP

Berkshire FHS
Mr. J. Gurnett, 34, Hawkesbury Drive, Fords Farm, Calcot, Reading, Berkshire RG3 5ZR

Birmingham & Midland Society for Genealogy & Heraldry
Mrs. J. Watkins, 92 Dimmingsdale Bank, Birmingham, West Midlands B32 1ST

Bristol and Avon FHS
Mrs. K. Kearsey, 135, Cotham Brown, Bristol BS6 6AD

Buckinghamshire FHS
Mrs. E. McLaughlin, 18 Rudds Lane, Haddenham, Aylesbury, Bucks.

Cambridgeshire FHS
Mrs. P. Close, 56 The Street, Kirtling, Newmarket, Cambridgeshire CB8 9PB

FHS of Cheshire
Mrs. D. Foxcroft, 5 Gordon Ave., Bromborough, Wirral, Merseyside

Cleveland FHS
Mr. A. Sampson, 1, Oxgang Close, Redcar TS10 4ND

Cornwall FHS
Mr. M. Martin, Chimneypots, Sunny Corner, Cusgarne, Truro, Cornwall TR4 8SE

Cumbria FHS
Mrs. M. Russell, 32 Granada Road, Denton, Manchester M34 2LJ

Derbyshire FHS
Mrs. P. Marples, 15, Elmhurst Road, Forest Town, Mansfield, Nottinghamshire NG19 0EV

Devon FHS
Miss V. Bluett, 63, Old Laira Road, Laira, Plymouth, Devon PL3 5BL

Doncaster FHS
Miss E Whitehouse, 7 Sherburn Close, Skellow, Doncaster, S. Yorkshire DN 6 8LG

Dorset
see Somerset & Dorset

Durham
see Northumberland & Durham

Essex FHS
Mr. C. Lewis, 48, Walton Road, Frinton-on-Sea, Essex CO13 0AG

Folkestone & District
Mrs. M. Criddle, 22, Church Road, Cheriton, Folkestone, Kent

Gloucestershire FHS
Mr. J. Vaughan, 1, Roxton Drive, The Reddings, Cheltenham, Glos. GL51 6SQ

Hampshire Genealogical Society
Mrs. J. Hobbs, 12, Ashling House, Chidham Walk, Havant, Hants. PO9 1DY

Herefordshire FHS
Mrs. V. Hadley, 255, Whitecross Road, Hereford HR4 0LT

Hertfordshire F&PHS
Mrs. J. Laidlaw, 155, Jessop Road, Stevenage, Herts.

Kent FHS
Mrs. H. Lewis, 17, Abbots Place, Canterbury, Kent CT1 2AH

North West Kent FHS
Miss J. M. Biggs, 39, Nightingale Road, Petts Wood, Orpington, Kent BR5 1BH

Lancashire Family History and Heraldry Society
Mr. R. Hampson, 7, Margaret Street, Oldham, Lancs. OL2 8RP

Leicestershire FHS
Miss S. Brown, 25, Homecroft Drive, Packington, Ashby de la Zouche, Leics.

Society for Lincolnshire History & Arch. (Family History Section)
Mrs. E Robson, 135 Baldertongate, Newark, Notts. NG24 1RY

Liverpool & District FHS
Mr. H. Culling, 11, Lisburn Lane, Tuebrook, Liverpool

East of London FHS
Mr. A. Polybank, Flat 2, 193-7 Mile End Road, London E1 4AA

Isle of Man FHS
Miss P. Killip, 9, Sandringham Drive, Onchan, IOM

Manchester & Lancashire FHS
Mr. E. Crosby, 32, Bournlea Avenue, Burnage, Manchester M19 1AF

Central Middlesex FHS
Mrs E. V. Pirie, 44, Dorchester Avenue, North Harrow, Middlesex HA2 7AU

North Middlesex FHS
Miss J. Lewis, 15, Milton Road, Walthamstow, London E17

West Middlesex FHS
Mrs. M. Morton, 92, Avondale Ave, Staines, Middlesex TW18 2NF

Norfolk & Norwich GS
Miss C. Hood, 293, Dereham Road, Norwich NR2 3TH

Northamtonshire FHS
Miss L. Wesley, 56, Gloucester Crescent, Delapre, Northampton NN4 9PR

Northumberland & Durham FHS
Mr. J. K. Brown, 33, South Bend, Brunton Park, Newcastle-on-Tyne, NE3 5TR

Nottinghamshire FHS
Miss S. M. Leeds, 35, Kingswood Road, West Bridgford, Nottingham NG2 7HT

Oxfordshire FHS
Mrs. V. Lee, Speedwell, North Moreton, Oxon. OX11 9BG

Peterborough & District FHS
Mrs. C. Newman, 106, London Road, Peterborough, Cambs PE2 9BY

Sheffield & District FHS
Mrs. E. Furey, 58, Stumperlowe Crescent Road, Sheffield, S10 3PR

Shropshire FHS
Mrs. G. Lewis, 15, Wesley Drive, Oakengates, Telford, Shropshire TF2 0DZ

Somerset & Dorset FHS
Mr. T. P. Farmer, Bru-Lands, Marston Road, Sherborne, Dorset DT9 4BL

Staffordshire
see Birmingham

Suffolk Genealogy Society
Mrs. K. Bardwell, 2, Fern Avenue, North Oulton Broad, Lowestoft, Suffolk

East Surrey FHS
Mrs. M. Brackpool, 370, Chipstead Valley Road, Coulsdon, Surrey CR3 3BF

West Surrey FHS
Mrs. M. Taylor, 60, Ashley Road, Farnborough, Hants. GU14 7HB

Sussex FHS
Mrs. B. Mottershead, 44 The Green, Southwick, Sussex, BN4 4FR

Waltham Forest FHS
Mrs. J. Thompson, 49 Tavistock Avenue, Walthamstow, London E17 6HR

Warwickshire
see Birmingham

Wiltshire FHS
Mrs. M. R. Moore, 17, Blakeney Avenue, Nythe, Swindon, Wilts. SN3 3NE

Windsor, Slough & District FHS
Mrs. J. Catlin, 2, Fair-croft, Slough SL2 1HJ, Bucks.

Woolwich & District FHS
Ms. S. Highley, 4, Church Road, Bexleyheath, Kent

Worcestershire
see Birmingham

Yorks. Arch. Society (Family and Pop. Studies Section)
Mrs. B. Shimwell, 24, Holt Park Road, Adel, Leeds LS16 7QS

East Yorks. FHS
Mr. R. E. Walgate, 9 Stepney Grove, Scarborough, North Yorks. YO12 5DF

York FHS
Mrs. F. Foster, 1, Ouse Lea, Shipton Road, York YO3 6SA

****

International Society for British Genealogy and Family History
POB 20425
Cleveland OH 44120

National Genealogical Society
4527 17th St N.
Arlington VA 22207-2363

Chicago Genealogical Society
POB 1160
Chicago IL 60690

Florida Genealogical Society
POB 18624
Tampa FL 33679

International Genealogy Fellowship of Rotarians
5721 Antietam Dr.
Sarasota FL 33581

Ventura County Genealogical Society
POB DN
Ventura CA 93002

Houston Genealogical Forum
POB 271469
Houston TX 77277-1469

Jefferson County Genealogical Society
POB 174
Oskaloosa KS 66066

English Interest Group, Minnesota Genealogical Society
9009 Northwood Circle
New Hope MN 55427

Santa Barbara County Genealogical Society
POB 1174
Goleta CA 93116

Genealogical Association of Sacramento
1230 42nd Ave
Sacramento CA 95822

Utah Genealogical Society
POB 1144
Salt Lake City UT 84110

Seattle Genealogical Society
POB 549
Seattle WA 98111

APPENDIX D

REGIONAL TOURIST BOARDS OF ENGLAND

London
British Tourist Authority Information Center, 64 St. James's Street, London SW1; tel: 01-499 9325

London Tourist Board, 26 Grosvenor Gardens, London SW1; tel: 01-730 0791

NOTE: For personal callers only, the L.T.B. has bureaux on Platform 15 at Victoria Station, Harrods Fourth Floor, Selfridges Ground Floor and Heathrow Central Underground Station.

South East England Tourist Board
Chevoit House, 4-6 Monson Road, Tunbridge Wells, Kent; tel: 0892 40766

Southern Tourist Board
Old Town Hall, Leigh Road, Eastleigh, Hampshire; tel: 0703 616027

Isle of Wight Tourist Board
21 High Street, Newport, Isle of Wight; tel: 0983 524343 or 525141

West Country Tourist Board
Trinity Court, 37 Southernhay East, Exeter, Devon; tel: 0392 76351

West Midlands
Heart of England Tourist Board, POB 15, Worcester; tel: 0905 29511

South Midlands
Thames and Chilterns Tourist Board, POB 10, 8 The Market Place, Abingdon, Oxon.; tel: 0235 22711

East Anglia Tourist Board
14 Museum Street, Ipswich, Suffolk; tel: 0473 214211

East Midlands Tourist Board
Exchequergate, Lincoln; tel: 0522 31521

Lancashire, Cheshire & Peak District
North West Tourist Board, The Last Drop Village, Bromley Cross, Bolton, Lancashire; tel: 0204 591511

Yorkshire & Humberside Tourist Board
312 Tadcaster Road, York, North Yorkshire; tel: 0904 707961

Isle of Man Tourist Board
13 Victoria Street, Douglas, Isle of Man; tel: 0624 4323

Cumbria, Northumbria & Durham
Northumbria Tourist Board, 9 Osborne Terrace, Newcastle-upon-Tyne; tel: 0632 817744

British Tourist Authority Offices in the USA
680 5th Ave
New York NY 10019
tel: (212) 581-4700

612 S Flower St
Los Angeles CA 90017
tel: (213) 623 8196

John Hancock Center
875 N Michigan Ave #3320
Chicago IL 60611
tel: (312) 787- 0490

These offices can supply general information, maps, etc.

APPENDIX E

AMERICAN/ENGLISH VOCABULARY LIST

AMERICAN	ENGLISH	AMERICAN	ENGLISH
baggage room	left luggage office	odometer	mileometer
band-aid	elastoplast/ plaster	one way ticket	single ticket
		outlet/socket	power point
bathtub	bath	pantie hose	tights
billfold	wallet	parking lot	car park
broil	grill	pass (vehicle)	overtake
call collect	reverse charges	pavement	road
		period	full-stop
carnival	fair	pullman	sleeping-car
check (restaurant)	bill	purse/pocket book	handbag
chips	crisps	raincoat	mac/macintosh
closet	wardrobe	restroom	cloakroom/toilet or lavatory
dessert	pudding/ sweet		
divided hwy	dual carriageway	round trip ticket	return ticket
down town	city centre	sales clerk	shop- assistant
druggist	chemist	schedule	timetable
elevator	lift	sidewalk	pavement
fall	autumn	stand in line	queue
faucet	tap	stop light	traffic light
freeway	motorway	two weeks	fortnight
French fries	chips	windshield	windscreen
garbage can	dustbin	wire	telegram
directory assistance	directory enquiries	with or without (milk/ cream)	black or white?
janitor	caretaker	yard	garden
lawyer	solicitor	zero	nought
legal holiday	bank holiday	zip code	postal code
liquor	spirits		
long distance	trunk call		
lost & found	lost property		
mailbox	pillar box		
make reserva- tion	book		
movie theater	cinema		
news dealer	newsagent		

APPENDIX F

MEDIEVAL LATIN WORD LIST

abatio	annulment	anno domini	in the year of our Lord
abavia/us	2nd great-grand-mother/father	annonymus/a	stillborn child
abortivus	prematurely born	Annuntiatio	the Annunciation (March 25)
accasatus	resident tenant		
acuarius	needlemaker	apothecarius	pharmacist
addico	I promise	apprenticius	apprentice
adolescens	young man	approbatio testamenti	probate of test-ament
adoperatio	working; appli-cation	archiator	doctor
adoptivus	adopted	arcularius	carpenter
adprimas	first of all	argentum	cash
adultus	young boy	armentarius	herdsman
aedilis	architect	asarcha	Lent
aetas	age	Assumptio	Feast of the Assumption (Aug. 15)
aetatis	aged		
agellarius	husbandman		
agenda	mass for the dead	Assumptio a Salvatoris	Ascension Day
agnomentum	surname	atava	grandmother
agricola	farmer	aucarius	gooseherd
aldermannus	ealdorman, no-bleman	aurifaber	goldsmith
		avia	grandmother
alius	the other (of 2)	avuncula	aunt
alleluia clau-sum	Septuagissima Sunday	ava/us	grandmother/father
alutarius	both (of this parish)	avunculus mag-nus/major	great-uncle
amicus	kinsman		
amita	aunt on father's side	baccalaureus	bachelor
		ballistrarius	gunsmith
amita magna	grandfather's sister	baptizatio	baptism
		barcarius	shipmaker
androchia	dairymaid	bastardus	bastard
anella	old woman	beda	prayer
anime	masses for the dead	belmannus	bell-ringer
		bercarius	shepherd, tan-ner
Animarum commemoratio	All Soul's Day (Nov. 2)		
		bidens	sheep

76

bigamia	2nd marriage	causarius	hatmaker
bijuges (pl.)	crockery	celebs	single or widowed
bolstera	bolster		
bondus	head of house-hold	cellarium	store-room
		cellarius	butler
boverius	oxherd	cimiterius	mason
bovicula	heifer	(dies) cene ad	
boviculus	bullock	mandatum	Maundy Thursday
bostio	plough-boy	cerefactor	chandler
bramum	well, pit	cervisiarius	ale-house keeper
Brandones	1st Sunday in Lent	Charisma	Whit Sunday
		chirothecator	glover
braciator	brewer	chirugus	surgeon
bubularius	oxherd	Circumcisio	
bubulcus	oxherd, plough-man	Domini	The Circumcision (January 1)
buscarius	butcher	cista	coffin
butularius	butter	cistarius	box-maker
buttarius	cooper	cistator	treasurer
buistarius	box-maker	Clausio Pasche	Sunday after Easter
chivalerus	knight	Clausio	
cabo	stallion	Pentecostes	Trinity Sunday
caelebs	see celebs	claustrarius	locksmith
caligator	hosier	coffinarius	basket-maker
camera	room, chamber	cognatus	cousin, kinsman
campana	bell, clock	comes	earl, count
campanitor	bell-ringer	commater	godmother
campus	field	compater	godfather
campester	peasant	Conceptio Beati	
Canderlaria	Candlemas (Feb-ruary 2nd)	Virginis	Feast of the Conception (December 8)
candelifex	chandler		
capa	cape, hooded cloak	conjug:	married
		connutrucius	foster-brother
carbo	coal	contractio	marriage contract
carbonarius	coal-miner		
carecarius	carter, plough-man	Conversatio	
		Sancti Pauli	Conversion of St Paul (Jan 25)
caretta	cart		
carnificium	shambles, meat market	convicina	neighbor
		coppa	hen
carnlevaria	Shrove Tuesday	coquina	kitchen
carnisbrevium	beginning of Lent		furniture
		cordifer	rope-maker
carrucator	ploughman	cordonarius	leather-maker
casale	village	(festum dies)	
caskettum	casket	corpus Christi	Thursday after Trinity
cassatio	nullification		
catabulum	pigsty	cotuca	tunic
catallum &	chattel, move-	cotarius	cottager
capitale	able goods	crastinum	tomorrow
Cathedra,		croftum	plot of land
Festum Sancti		crumenarius	pursemaker
Petri in,	St. Peter's Chair (Feb 22)	cudarus	forester
		cutellarius	cutler

cum	by, with		domificator	carpenter, builder
coupa	cup, bowl			
cupbordum	cupboard		dos	dower, endowment
cutissima	curtain		drapa	cloth
custor	sacristan		draperus	draper
			dressura	serving-board
d.s.p.	died without issue		ducena	twelve
			dum	when, since
d.v.m.	died while mother living			
			eductio carruce	Plough Monday (1st after Epiphany)
d.v.p.	died while father living			
			eloco	give in marriage
dayaria	dairy		emptum	purchase
decada	ten		engia (pl)	mortgage
decennarius	tithing-man		enopola	taverner
decima (festum)	tithing		entalliator	stone-carver
Decollationis Sancti Johanni Baptisti	Beheading of St John (Aug 29)		ephestris	surcoat
			ephipparius	saddler
			Epiphania Domini	Epiphany (Jan 6)
deducator ferarum	gamekeeper		equus	horse
defensiva	fence		eques	knight
denarius	penny		ergo	therefore
derelicta	widow		ericetum	heath, moor
desponsatio	betrothal, marriage		eruptio	spring of water
			escaria	sideboard
didymus	twin		escarium	manger
dies Dominica	Sunday		et	and
dies Soles	Sunday		(festum) exaltionis Sancti Crucis	Holy Cross Day (Sept 14)
dies Lune	Monday			
dies Martis	Tuesday			
dies Mercurii	Wednesday		excusor	printer
dies Wodenis	Wednesday		executor testamenti	executor of will
dies Jovis	Thursday			
dies Veneris	Friday		exheredatus	disinherited
dies Veneris Bonus/Sancta	Good Friday		exlex	outlaw
			expensa	storeroom
dies Sabbati (-nus)	Saturday		extravagus	vagrant
dies Saturni	Saturday		faber cupri	coopersmith
digamus	twice married		faber ferrarius	blacksmith
disjugata	unmarried woman		faber lignarius	joiner
dispunctuo	settle accounts		faber scriniarius	cabinet-maker
deviso	bequeath		fabrica	forge
doga	wainscot		falcata	measure of a meadow
domesticalia	household goods			
domus	house		famulia	household
domus brasinea	brew-house		fantulus/ fantula	little boy or girl
domus carbonum	coal-house			
domus cervisiana	ale-house			
domus feni	barn		fenestra	window
domus porcorum	pigsty		fena	hay-fields
domus vaccarum	cow-shed			

ferdingus	farthing (1/4 penny)	grabatum	skirt
feria	festival, weekday	gramen	pasturage
feria prima	Sunday	grammaticulus	schoolboy
feria secunda etc.	Monday	grana	grain
ferma	farm	granarium	granary
ferocia	quilt, mattress	grangia decimalis	tithe-barn
ferreum	horse-shoe	grotus	groat (coin)
ferrifaber	iron-smith		
fidatio	betrothal	habedassarius	haberdasher
fidejussor	godparent	hebdomada	week
filius	son	heres	heir
filius in lege	son-in-law	histrio	player, minstrel
filius naturalis	bastard	homo	man
filiaster	stepson, son-in-law	hordeum	barley
filiastra	step-daughter	horilogium	clock
filiola/us	god-daughter/son	horrea	barn
fiscalia	taxes	hortus	garden
flecciator	fletcher	hortulanus	gardener
florinus	gold coin	hospitium	household
focarium	hearth	hostillarius	inn-keeper
fons	well	humatus	buried
foramen	window-pane	hundredum	hundred (division of county)
fossor	digger, miner	husbandus	husbandman
fotherator	furrier	hypante	Candlemas (February 2)
frater	brother		
frater in lege	brother-in-law	ignotus	illegitimate
fratruelusa/us	niece/nephew	imbrevio	to record in writing
frethum	hedge	impendo	give, spend
fritha	woodland, pasture	impraegnata	pregnant before marriage
frumentum	wheat	imprimis	in the first place
frunitor	tanner	inconjugatus	unwed
fugarius	drover	indigentia (pl)	necessaries
fullaticus	fuller	infrascriptus	written below
furlongus	furlong (1/8 mile)	inhumatio (festum) innocentium	burial Holy Innocents (Dec 28)
Galilea	porch of church	insinuo	register a will
galitarius	shoemaker	intratio	entry (into a building)
ganata	bowl	ire (eo)	go
garba	sheaf (of corn)	ita quod	on condition that
garcifer	servant	iter	path
gardinum	garden, orchard	item	next (on list), also
gardinarius	gardener		
gavella	family holding		
geldum	tax		
gemelli	twins		
gilda (terra)	guild	jakkum	sleeveless tunic
glebalis	glebe-land		

jejunium guadragesimale	Lent
(caput) jejuni	Ash Wednesday
judex	judge
juramentus exhibitum fuit	certificate (of burial in wool)
jus	right, due
juvencula	girl
juvenis	young man
juxta	according to
laboratio	ploughing
laboro ad	work at
laicus	layman
lana	wool or wool-tax
lanatus	'buried in wool'
lanifex	clothier
landa	untilled land
lapis	stone (weight)
lararium	closet
lardaria	larder
largitas	width
latro	thief
lautumus	mason
lectus	bed-clothes, bed
legatio	legacy
lego in manus	bequeath
laetare	third Sunday of Lent
liber	book, freeman
libra	pound (weight or money)
lignarius	joiner
lignum	wood
ligniscissor	woodcutter
linea	linen cloth or garment
macellaria	meat-market
macellarius	butcher
macerio	mason
magister	master (of school or trade)
major	adult
mala	rent, mail
malarium	orchard
malluvium	wash-basin
maunda	hamper
mare	sea
maria	lake
marium	moor, marsh
maritagium	marriage
maritellus	husband
mater	mother

mater meretrix	illegitimate mother
matrimonium	dowry
mauseolum	coffin, tomb
medicus	physician
mensa	food, table
meta	boundary
methodus	road
migratio ad Christum/Dominum	die
miles	knight
mille	thousand
mobile	movable goods
modius	a peck (measure)
molendinum	mill
molendinum venti	windmill
molitarius corlii	leather-worker
morganaticus	morgantic (marriage)
multrix	milk-maid
mulier	wife
multardus	shepherd
munimen	enclosure
murena	marsh
murus	wall
napiria	table linen
natalicium	birthday, Saint's day
natalicium Dominicum	Christmas
nativitas	birthplace
nativitatis Domini	Christmas
nativitas beate Marie	Birth of the Blessed Mary (Dec 8)
nepos	nephew
neptis	niece
netrix	spinster
nomen proprium	baptismal name
novercarius (testamentum)	stepfather
noncupative facto	oral will
nubo	give in marriage
nubo me	wed
obiit	died
obiit sine prole	died without issue
opus	work
orphanus	orphan

80

ovis	sheep
ovianus	shepherd
pactum	contract, lease
pagus	village
pajettus	page, servant
pallium	funeral shroud
(Dominica) in palmis	Palm Sunday
palus	marsh, fence
pandoxatorium	ale-house
panis	bread
palna	roof-timber storey of house
pannus	cloth, garment
paraphernalia	married woman's property
(dies) paracevensis	Good Friday
parentalia	family, kin
parochia	parish, parish church
Pascha	Easter Sunday
Pascha Album	Low Sunday
Pascha Minus dies Lune	Palm Sunday
Paschalis	Easter Monday
pascua & pastura	pasture
patella	bowl, pan
pater	father
pater in lege	father-in-law
patrinus	godfater
patruus magnus	great-uncle
pauso	rest, die
peciata	peck (measure)
pecunia	money
pelvis	basin
penarium	cupboard
pendilium	curtain
Pentecoste	Pentecost
penulator	furrier
per	by, on (day of the week)
peregrinus	pilgrim
perempticius	apprentice
(dies Luna) perjurata	second Monday after Easter
persinctus	boundary
persolutio	payment in full
pestilentia	the Plague
pictor	painter
pilleus	cap
pincernarius	butler
piscenarius	fishmonger

platula	plate
plus	more
polis	city
polata	pole (measure of land)
pomarium	orchard
pondus	weight, pound
porcarius	swineherd
porcus	pig
posteritas	descendants
purcingtus	boundary
preco	watchman
precontractus	precontract (of marriage)
pregnatus	pregnant
prehibitus	aforesaid
prememoratus	previously mentioned
presbyter	old man, priest
prevolentia	antecedent will
prida	mortgage
primogenitor	first-born
prevignus	stepson
pro	because of, for
proava/us	great-grand-mother/ father
procreamen	offspring
proles	offspring
proles spuria	illegitimate offspring
propinquitas	kinsfolk
provincia	shire, county
pucella & puella	girl
puer	boy
puerpera	mother
Purificans	Candlemas (February 2)
quadragesima (Dominica)	Lent
quadragesime	first Sunday in Lent
quadravus	great-great-grandfater
quadriga	wagon
quasimodo geniti	Low Sunday
quondam	formerly
quoniam	since, because
Ramispalme	Palm Sunday
relicta	widow

(dies Dominica)
reliquiarium   Relic Sunday
                  (first after
                  July 7)
resurrectio
  Dominica   Easter Sunday
roparius   rope-maker
rusticus   peasant
(dies)
  Sabbatinus   Saturday
(dies)
  Sabbatainus
sanctus   Holy Saturday
sacerdos   priest
sarrator   sawyer
shamellum   shambles, meat
                   market
shira   shire
scholarius   scholar
scilicet   namely
scotus de
  capite   poll-tax
sculptor
  lapidum   mason
scyphus   cup
se   him
seculum   worldly affairs
sepiens   hay-maker
Septuagesima   Septuagesima
                  Sunday
sepultura   buried
sericum   silk
servitor &
  serviens   servant
sestertius   shilling
silvacedus   woodcutter
simplex   of low rank
sobrina/us   cousin on
                   mother's side
socius   fellow
solemnia
  nuptiarum   to celebrate a
                   marriage
solidum   undivided
                   property
solidus   shilling
soror   sister
sororius   sister's husband
spera   sideboard
spondea rotans   trundle bed
sponsalia   banns of
                   marriage
sponsus/a   spouse
statim   at once
stuprata   pregnant out of
                   wedlock

sudarium   napkin
suarium   shroud
sus   swine
sutor
  caligarius   hosier
sutor
  chirothecarius glover
sutor vestarius   tailor
suus   own

taberna   tavern, inn
tabernio   inn-keeper
tabula   board, shutter
tabula mansalis   table
tallia   tally
tannator   tanner
tantellus   cousin
tector   thatcher
tenementum   house
testamentum   will, bequest
textator   weaver
tia   maternal aunt
traditio &
  tradux   inheritance
transfiguratio
  Domini   Transfiguration
                  (August 6)
tumba   tomb
tunica   coat

ulna   ell (measure of
                   length)
ulterior   additional
unicus/a   unmarried man/
                   woman
ustilmenta   household goods
uxor   Mrs., wife

vedovus   widower
viciatus   bastard
vidua   widow
vincula Sancti
  Petri   Saint Peter's
                  Chains (Aug 1)

warda   guardianship

xped   christened